BRAIN PAIN

The true story of a family with overwhelming mental disorders that will inspire you to overcome your toughest problems

by
J. A. Gorczyca

DEDICATION

*To mom – who raised six children, lived a life of care and
compassion, and left a legacy of unconditional love.*

We love you,

*Mary Ann, Billy, Joe
Janice, Kathy, John*

PROLOGUE

Each year, over 60 million people – 26 percent of the U.S. population ages 18 and older – experience some type of mental disorder.

Mental illness spares none – the rich and the poor; the old and the young; all races, all nationalities.

Some celebrities have talked openly about their struggles with depression and other psychiatric disorders. And the recent suicide of comedian Robin Williams helped remind people that mental illness can affect anyone, regardless of their age, wealth, status or apparent disposition.

There are also cultural differences that make it challenging to understand when someone really needs help. What some people may call extreme sadness could actually be clinical depression.

Popular movies and news coverage of violence committed by people with mental illness help perpetuate negative stereotypes. In reality, less than 5 percent of violent crimes are committed by people who have a mental disorder, according to the American Psychiatric Association.

Still, the stigma remains a major obstacle for people coping with mental disorders. Less than a third of people who have a mental disorder receive treatment. Some hesitate for fear that others will treat them differently.

It could happen to you – or someone in your family.

Let me tell you about my family.

TABLE OF CONTENTS

CHAPTER 1

In the News: Naked Lady on the Freeway

It was March 7, 2016. I was driving on Highway 290 in Houston, Texas. Up ahead the traffic was stalled and I could see flashing red lights. Not necessarily an uncommon sight in Houston, where the traffic is heavy and there are certainly many accidents on the road every day.

But this one was different. As I approached the scene of the accident, I could see on the opposite side of the freeway that there were two cars which had major damage – looked like a bad crash, but did not see any bodies on the road nor anyone being carried on a stretcher.

And then I saw one of the most bizarre things that I have ever witnessed. About a hundred feet down the road was an eighteen wheeler parked on the freeway with a naked woman sitting atop the truck!

This was not just any naked woman… she was a very obese woman (must have weighed at least 350 pounds) with wild, frazzled hair. She was looking up to the sky, swinging her arms, and yelling out to the police officers that were trying to reach her.

Simply put, I was shocked. Her appearance and behavior were outlandish – both scary and pathetic at the same time. What was her story? What caused her to do something like this? What was her illness?

****

Unfortunately, we frequently hear of stories in the news that shock us, anger us, scare us, or make us feel sad, sympathetic, and helpless.

Many times, there is no one to help those with mental disorders. They never get to see a doctor; they never get medication; they never get admitted to a hospital for psychiatric care; they never get to live in a special care home. Instead, they often end up in prison.

During March, 2015, Mark Joyella of TV Newser interviewed CNN's Anderson Cooper about his recent report on America's overwhelming number of people in our prisons who are mentally ill.

Anderson Cooper said it was "eye-opening" when he talked to some of the inmates at Chicago's Cook County Jail. They described our prisons as a place to just 'dump people' with mental illness.

"It's great that they receive some treatment in jail," Cooper told TV Newser. "But there has to be a better way to help people struggling with mental illness that doesn't depend on them committing a criminal offense."

Cooper talked with inmates – some of them have never committed a violent crime, yet they have spent more than half their lives locked up. Sheriff Thomas Dart, who is a strong advocate for reform, recently told The New York Times "the same society that abhorred the idea that we lock people up in mental hospitals, now we lock people up in jails."

CHAPTER 2

INSANITY: MY GREAT GRANDMA – KATHERINE

Myth:

CRAZY PEOPLE JUST NEED TO BE PUT AWAY – THEY ARE DANGEROUS

I was only 6 years old. It was summertime and a really, really hot afternoon in St. Louis (that's where I grew up).

I sat in the back seat of my dad's 1954 Chevy along with my sister Mary Ann and my grandma (she always did special things for me). My dad was driving and my mom rode in the front with him.

We were going to see my great grandma – my mom's grandma. She lived in a hospital (which I really did not understand). It was the St. Louis State Hospital (I heard people call it the insane asylum). I held my grandma's hand as we walked into the hospital. It smelled really bad in there. There was this really big room with about a hundred beds in there! Just row after row of beds.

The room was full of women who looked really sick. Not because they had broken bones or were bleeding, but they looked hungry and weak. I saw my great grandma and ran to her. She smiled at me and gave me a big hug. My mom told me her name was Katherine but I called her great grandma. She had pure white hair that was very long; her skin was very wrinkly like prunes; her teeth were sort of yellow and black and she was dressed in a night gown.

She then asked my dad, "Did you all come in the machine?" He said "yes." Then my mom told me that my great grandma was talking about the car (sounded very funny to call it a machine). Then she said that she wanted to go to the farm. I had never been to a farm, but I saw pictures of farms in my books at home.

My grandma told me that her mom grew up on a farm in Kampsville, Illinois. Sounded like it would be a lot of fun to have cows and chickens and pigs. I wanted to go too. But my grandma told her that it was too far. My great grandma started to cry.

I did not understand why she could not live at home with my grandma and grandpa. Why did she have to live in a hospital? (This did not make sense to me). I had made her a picture from my coloring book at home that I brought to her. She gave me another hug. Even though she kind of smelled funny, I'm glad she hugged me. It made her happy.

****

I don't remember a lot else about my visits to see my great grandma. She died when I was 8 years old – she was 92! (I didn't think that anybody could live to be 92 years old). As I got older, my mom told me more about my great grandma. She had some type of nervous breakdown when she was in her early 40s. There was nothing the doctors could do to help her except put her in the state hospital along with other people who had problems in their mind (mental illness).

Right after my great grandma died, I heard some man on TV say "crazy people just need to be put away – they are dangerous." I asked my mom why he said that. She said "that man was wrong and that some people just don't understand. People who have a mental illness really need someone to take care of them because they are sick."

I remember that my great grandma was gentle and loving. I always wished that she could have gotten better and come home with us. But at least I know that she is in heaven (my mom and grandma said so).

****

As a child, I had a very limited view and understanding about mental illness. I'm sure that my parents and grandparents wanted to protect me from many of the horrors that took place – in the asylums, in the prisons, on the streets, and even in family homes.

There was a movie released in 1948 entitled The Snake Pit. In this psychological drama, Virginia Cunningham (Olivia de Havilland) is confused upon finding herself in a mental hospital, with no memory of her arrival at the institution. Tormented by delusions and unable to even recognize her husband, she is treated by her doctor, who is determined to get to the root of her mental illness. As her treatment progresses, flashbacks depict events in Virginia's life that may have contributed to her instability. This movie depicts some of the deplorable and inhumane conditions that were very common in mental institutions.

Letter to Great Grandma

Although my great grandma Katherine has passed away, I still think about her and never want her to be forgotten. I would like to share these thoughts with her.

Dear Great Grandma,

I was only a young boy when I knew you. I do remember seeing sadness in your eyes. I did not understand – I was too young. But now I understand so much more. I wish that you could have had a better life. I am sure that you endured much suffering. My heart aches for you.

I loved your daughter, my grandma, so very much. She was kind and funny and loved children. I am sure that you instilled these wonderful traits in her – while you were still well. I could see her love for you – you must have been a good mom.

My comfort is knowing that you are in heaven. You now have no tears, no fears, and no hurt. You are at peace. I rejoice to know that I will see you in heaven – as a beautiful woman who is now full of joy.

I love you,

Joe

What is happening in our world today?

In April 2015, Nicholas Perpitch, ABC News-Australia, reported on horrific conditions that still exist in some mental health facilities.

Mr. Perpitch reports that people with disabilities have been found repeatedly raped, severely neglected, with broken bones and left humiliated in their own feces for many hours.

There are witnesses who gave many examples of assault by the staff who had been responsible to care for people with disabilities in group homes and mental health centres.

Women with Disabilities WA coordinator Rayna Lamb said the abuse of disabled people was very often underreported or not reported at all - mostly because the victims were not believed or could not communicate what had happened to them.

"It's so common," she said. "On one hand, it's assumed no one would treat a person with a disability badly. People just want to care for people with disabilities. But we live in a society where the attitude to disability means predators know that they can attack us, that they can abuse us, that they can treat us like shit because who is going to believe it?"

Ms Lamb said non-verbal people were particularly vulnerable because often when they expressed their anguish through actions, such as banging their heads or screaming; it was wrongly interpreted as part of their disability.

Mr. Perpitch also reported about a group of women from the disability advocacy group Bolshy Divas who gave collective evidence on forty cases where disabled people had been severely beaten or raped. This group told about a twelve year old girl who came home from a school camp for disabled children with a deep cut to her vagina. The police investigated but the child could not speak and was unable to explain what happened to her.

"Basically, there's no accountability and it goes nowhere," Bolshy Divas' Samantha Connor said.

"Institutional settings are just breeding grounds for people to be deprived of independent advocacy," Ms Connor said. Based on available figures, ninety percent of women with intellectual disabilities were sexually abused.

An executive of Advocare, Sharon Richards, said that the rights of people with disabilities are highly ignored.

She told about an eighty year old woman who was found with bruises and a badly fractured femur that had not been attended to. Another woman was allegedly left with an injury to the top of her head; she had been hit with the buzzer used to call staff.

"They are very vulnerable and unable, more often than not, to speak up for themselves," Ms Richards said.

"They are worried about retribution, and, instead of dealing with the issue they tend to move residential facility or just sweep it under the carpet."

CHAPTER 3

INTELLECTUAL DISABILITY: MY BROTHER – BILLY

> ### *Myth:*
> ### MENTALLY RETARDED CHILDREN DON'T HAVE FEELINGS OR EMOTIONS

I was 10 years old.

My brother Billy was the third child born in our family of six children (I was the oldest). Billy was special. He had a lot of problems when he was first born. His eyes were crossed, he was missing a finger on his right hand, he could not urinate normally (his penis was not formed properly) – and he was mentally retarded (the accepted term at that time). But I loved him so much!

Just after he was born, Billy was taken from my mom and placed in an infant care unit for observation. She was not able to see her new son and cried hysterically, "I want to see my baby – bring me my baby! Why can't I see my baby?" The nurses tried to reassure her that everything was going to be okay and that Billy just needed some special care before she could hold him.

But he was not going to be okay.

When he was only three years old, he started a series of operations to correct his eyes and to reconstruct his penis.

But he would always have only four fingers on his right hand – and he would always be mentally retarded.

When Billy was a little boy, I helped him go to the bathroom. I wiped his butt when he had a BM. As an adult, Billy still needs help getting his butt wiped. But also as an adult he can now urinate on his own, he can pull his pants up and down to go to the bathroom, he can feed himself, and he can follow basic directions to get in a car or van, go to class, or go to bed.

From the time he was born, my mom used to say that Billy was our 'angel on earth'. To this day, I still feel that way. Billy has had more influence on me than anyone else in my life. Because of him, I have learned what it means to care for others and to have compassion. I have learned how blessed that I am and never take anything for granted.

****

Billy loved dogs – and they loved him. While growing up, he used to share his sandwiches with our dog. He would take a bite and then give the dog a bite; they traded bites until it was gone. The funny thing is – Billy has been always the healthiest kid in our family!

He also loved music – especially rock and roll. He could not dance, but he would stand in place and rock back and forth to the beat of the music (it made him so happy).

A few of the favorite songs at that time were: Born to Be Wild (Steppenwolf), MacArthur Park (Richard Harris), Light My Fire (Jose Feliciano), American Woman (The Guess Who), Let It Be (The Beatles) – so many great songs and artists.

Believe it or not, his favorite thing was to go to school. He was fortunate to be able to attend a day program with other mentally retarded kids. A little yellow school bus picked him up each weekday and brought him home at the end of the day. Billy would stand by the front door in the morning and look for the little yellow school bus to come. He actually cried when there was no school on holidays, weekends, and snow days.

Unfortunately, Billy's vocabulary has always been very limited. So it was exciting for our family when he tried to say words – we would all clap and praise him. He pronounced my name 'Go-Go' since he could not say Joe. He pronounced his own name 'Ee-Ee' since he could not say Billy. It was so much fun at Christmas time when we would ask him what Santa Claus says. He would say 'Ho-Ho' and then smile very big!

Billy has always been a good eater. He ate so much but always stayed in good shape. Guess it was because he was always active - at school or walking around the house or in the backyard. My mom always had to keep an eye on food that she was preparing in the kitchen because Billy would sneak in and take food and then run to the other room before anybody saw him (funny thing is that his favorite foods were raw vegetables). Guess that's also why he has always been so healthy.

Another favorite trick of his was to go in the bathroom and take little strips of toilet paper. He would tear it up and make small paper balls and then stick one in his mouth to chew on and put the rest of them in his pocket to eat later. He was a real master at doing this.

There were also some bad things that happened.

****

I remember several times when kids in the neighborhood would come by the house and walk by our backyard to laugh and make fun of Billy – calling him names like 'retard'. It didn't matter how many of them there were or how big they were – finally I got my baseball bat and chased them off (the same kids never came back again). I have always tried to be Billy's protector – even to this day.

The great thing is that my friends were always very nice to Billy and tried to talk to him and play with him. I think a lot of other kids might have been nice to him if they understood (not many people seemed to understand about mental retardation – even grownups).

Sometimes, Billy did not know if something was dangerous. I remember a time when he was in the back yard. He sat down by a small window ledge near our basement. There was a wasp nest just above the window and he got nine wasp stings right on the top of his head! He did not know what happened and could not run to safety. One of our neighbors went with my mom to take Billy to the emergency room (we only had one car and my dad was at work).

I always wondered, "What is Billy thinking?" He was growing up physically, but he had the mind of a small toddler. He could only say a few words or point to what he wanted. He would never be able to really tell us what he was thinking. All I knew is that he was my brother and I loved him.

Even though Billy could not say the words of what he was thinking, somehow I knew. When I am with him, I can tell how he is feeling. If he is happy, he looks at me directly and smiles and wants to shake my hand. If he is sad or anxious, he looks away from me, does not smile, and does not reach out to me. When you are close to someone, it is amazing how strong non-verbal communication can be.

****

Whenever our family would go somewhere, I would walk with Billy and make sure that he did not fall – or run away (he could run pretty fast). I would hold his hand or his arm and make sure he would be safe.

I got a lot of weird stares from many people. They could see that Billy was different but looked at both of us with mixed reaction – some disapproving, some confused, some with disdain, but some with smiles of love and empathy. I would never stop holding onto Billy for the rest of my life.

****

Billy loved to be outside and walk around our backyard. Growing up, we had many beautiful flowers in our yard – climbing rose bushes, peonies, and the most wonderful lilac bushes. When the roses were first budding, Billy would pick some of the buds and carry them around with him and smell them. It finally got the best of him. One day, he was out in the yard and he started sneezing uncontrollably; we had no idea what was wrong. It actually got very serious and he started to panic. My mom got a ride with one of our neighbors and took him to the emergency room. Well, it turned out that Billy had put a rose bud up in his nostril and it got lodged way up high! We all had a good laugh after we knew he was going to be okay.

****

In St. Louis, there was an organization called SLARC (St. Louis Association for Retarded Children). My mom belonged to this organization and went to meetings to talk with other parents who had mentally retarded children. She told me that it really helped her to talk to other people and share ways of coping with all the challenges that go along with raising kids like Billy. This group also had a big picnic each summer when all the families got together to eat and play games. I also got to see many other kids who were mentally retarded yet looked very different from Billy. I remember several kids who had Down's syndrome (common term used was Mongoloid) and also one kid who had a very large head due to excess swelling in his brain (common term used was Watermelon head). It was a lot to take in but it helped me to understand that there were a lot of kids who were special like Billy.

I asked my mom about some of the things that the adults talked about at their meetings. She said, "Most people, even some parents with mentally retarded children, communicate a lot of wrong information." I asked, "Like what?" She replied, "Well, some people think that mentally retarded children don't have feelings or emotions. But, of course, these kids do have the same feelings and emotions as other children – they just can't express it the same." Yep, that made good sense to me.

What is happening in our world today?

In June 2015, Christina Veiga of the Miami Herald reported on students who faced charges for raping a mentally disabled girl.

In the report, Ms. Veiga told about a student who approached one of his classmates — a mentally disabled teenage girl in a job training program at North Miami Senior High.

He told her she was pretty and asked her to follow him; he led the girl to another boy who took her by the hand. The boy took her into a janitor's closet, closed the door, and turned out the lights. Then they were joined by three other boys who gang raped her, according to arrest forms.

The boys told her not to tell, but she did tell a security guard who saw them leaving the closet. The girl later told Miami-Dade school police the boys "forced her to perform oral, anal and vaginal sex acts."

Many of the teachers were extremely upset and worried about security – this was a campus with 2,400 students. But this horrific incident escaped public attention until it was announced that her four accused assailants would face trials in Miami-Dade County criminal court.

CHAPTER 4

ALCOHOLISM:
MY DAD – TONY

> *Myth:*
>
> **ALCOHOLICS NEED TO WANT**
> **HELP TO BE HELPED.**

I was 12 years old – our family was very close and loving. It's funny what things you remember as you look back on the early years.

One of the most memorable times was when my brother John was 5, my sister Janice was 3, and my sister Kathy was 2. I came home from playing baseball with my friends at the park. I always felt a special love for all my brothers and sisters – still do to this day. I think I remember more about when we were all young because those were the best of times.

Well, when I first walked into the back yard, I saw John, Janice, and Kathy all sitting in a circle by the back steps. Then I saw the biggest mess you could ever imagine – there on the ground was a huge pile of goop (best way to describe it) which included ketchup, mustard, mayo, milk, juice, eggs, and who knows what else!

I could hardly keep from laughing and at the same time thought "you guys are in big trouble!" I just said "so what are you guys doing?" John said, "We are making dinner for mom" (he was so proud). They had emptied the refrigerator, carried everything outside, and used sticks for their mixing spoons.

Amazingly, my mom took it all in stride. We got out the hose, washed it all out, and ate grilled cheese for dinner that night (no need for ketchup, mustard, or mayo). A typical day in a family with six kids.

****

I was in high school when many things began to change for our family, mostly because of my dad.

My dad was born a twin – the youngest of eight children. His dad owned and operated a tavern and store; he had severe drinking problems (bad career choice to own a tavern). My grandpa came to the U.S. from Poland and settled in St. Louis, MO. That's how our Gorczyca family got established in America.

I have always been very proud of my Polish heritage. The Polish people are known for their strong work ethic and love of family. I also enjoy eating kielbasa sausage and pierogies (Polish dumplings).

The name Gorczyca derives from 'mustard seed'. Always thought that was really cool since a mustard seed starts very small but grows up to be a very strong tree just as I hoped our family would grow to be strong.

Our last name was a challenge to pronounce for many people. On the first day of school every year, all the teachers would call roll. When they got to my name, they would usually say 'Joseph' – then pause and look up for help. Of course, I knew it was me. So, I gladly said my last name for them (pronounced Gor-si-ca). Actually kind of liked having a unique name. Until I got older, I thought that I might be the only Joe Gorczyca in the whole U.S. But thanks to the internet, I have discovered there are eight people with the name Joe Gorczyca.

My paternal grandpa died when my dad was young, so I never got to meet him. Just heard stories from my dad and my uncles and aunts. My dad had a tough childhood and quit school when he was 16 to help support his mom. He went to work as a package runner on a parcel delivery truck. Later on, he would become a truck driver for Sloan's Parcel Delivery (early day version of UPS). That would be his career.

****

My dad was a great athlete. I saw pictures and newspaper articles about him. During his early teens, he was the leading goal scorer in the St. Louis city soccer league. And that's saying something – St. Louis has a strong tradition of soccer, mainly because there were many eastern European immigrants who settled in St. Louis. He taught me a real love for the game.

He was also a fantastic baseball player. He was best known as a pitcher who could throw an amazing fast ball. He was even offered a tryout with the St. Louis Browns – an American league team. Unfortunately, he broke his arm just one month before the tryout and never recovered well enough to pitch. I always wondered how different his life (and my life) would have been if he became a major league pitcher.

****

As a kid, I had some wonderful times playing sports with my dad. We played a lot of baseball and 'whiffle ball' in the backyard. I even made our own baseball field with bases, a pitcher's mound, and an old table top that was set up behind home plate to serve as the strike zone, so you could play a game with only two people – did not even need a catcher.

It was always very competitive between me and my dad. When I turned 15, I was on the track team in high school and in really good shape (fond memories). Of course, my dad thought that he could still beat me in running so he challenged me to a race in our alley behind the house. We were really hyped up about this race to show who was the fastest. My little brother John was the judge. He stood about fifty yards away and yelled 'Go' for the start of the race. I sprinted off the starting line and was about twenty yards away – but I didn't see my dad anywhere. I looked back and saw him lying on the ground about two yards from the starting line. I went to check on him and he said, "Well, I guess I know who is the fastest now." He had strained the muscles in both his thighs during the first two steps that he took – we had a good laugh.

My dad's very favorite thing to do was barbecuing. He prepared his own special sauce (included a good portion of beer) and listened to Cardinals' baseball games on the radio. Barbecue hamburgers and hot dogs were a special treat for our family; every so often we had pork steaks (delicious). This seemed to be his way to relax and be an escape from the work week.

But the good times didn't last.

****

About this time in my life, my dad started to drink a lot of beer. After he got off work, he would go to a tavern with his work buddies to drink and talk. He would come home late from work most nights around 9:00 pm. When he got home, he would eat dinner that my mom had saved for him; then sit in his chair in the living room and fall asleep. About 11 p.m. my mom would wake him and tell him to go to bed.

It was really tough on my mom and all us kids. I always felt like I had a lot of responsibility from an early age. My dad was a very hard worker. It was really tough to support a family of six kids as a truck driver – plus the additional challenge of raising my brother Billy. My mom said that she thought it was all too much for my dad. She loved him very much and did her best to handle everything at home.

What made things worse was that my dad took on a second job on Friday and Saturday nights – working at a liquor store (again proved to be a very bad choice for a second job). He was just trying to provide for his family. But things at home got really bad.

Soon, my dad was not always home by 9 p.m. Sometimes, my mom would tell me to call the tavern and ask for my dad to see if he was there and ask him to come home. At first, she called the tavern, but that made him very mad.

Then the physical and verbal abuse started. My mom would be upset when my dad continued to get home late – obviously because he was drinking. He would yell at her and tell her that "he was the breadwinner and she had no right to complain." But then it got worse - he struggled with her and pushed her down.

How could this be happening! This is my dad. I know that he is a good man. I love him. Why is he doing this to my mom? I can't let him hurt her.

****

I will never forget the next time that my dad got into a fight with my mom. It torments me to this day. He came home late and was very drunk. I told all my brothers and sisters to go upstairs. My dad was very angry and began to grab my mom by her arms. I jumped in and pulled his arms away and wrestled him to the ground. He looked startled and yelled at me, "get away – this has nothing to do with you!" My dad was very strong, but I was able to hold him down on the ground. Fortunately, I was now his size and able to hold my own.

When this happened, my brothers and sisters had come downstairs when they heard all the noise. Everyone was crying and gathered around my mom. Our lives would never be the same.

During those years, our family had to keep many secrets. It didn't seem okay for anyone else to know that my dad had a drinking problem. That's what we always said (we never said that he was an alcoholic).

Except for my mom's friend Betty. She had a mentally retarded child also and got to be very good friends with my mom. She came to the house to visit my mom and I heard them talking. She told my mom, "Tony is an alcoholic. But he has to want help to be helped. It's up to him."

My mom was not sure what to do. She knew that my dad did not think that he had a drinking problem. According to him, "I just have a few drinks to help me relax. I work my butt off for this family. You're the one who needs help. You're the one who comes from a crazy family."

My mom talked to a priest at church. He told her, "Most alcoholics don't want help. They are sick and can't think rationally. They usually need someone to intervene." My mom and I both tried.

I wish that my dad would have gone for help – some group like Alcoholics Anonymous. But that didn't happen.

****

During my senior year in high school, I was trying so hard to help keep things together for our family. But I had my own activities going on: football, part-time job, dating, parties, and making plans for college. My dad always told me "make sure and get a good education; it's the most important thing you can do."

In his way, he reached out to me and tried his best to guide me. I still remember him telling me "you know that you can tell me anything. I have done everything that you have done and I have done everything that you have ever thought about doing."

Although there were special times when he would advise me and give me encouragement, there were the other times – the bad times. Like a Saturday night when he went to the tavern to 'have a few drinks'. It was midnight and my dad was still not home. This time my mom called the tavern and my dad yelled "I'll be home in a little while." It was obvious that he was drunk. My mom was very concerned about him driving home and told me to go get the car and drive it home (the tavern was about six blocks from our house). I walked to the tavern, got my dad's car, and drove home.

My mom and I waited up for my dad. About 1:30 a.m., we heard a noise outside. I rushed outside and found my dad lying in the driveway – his face was bleeding badly. I leaned down to help him and could see that his head was cut just above his right eyebrow. He looked up at me and mumbled, "Why did you take the car? Help me."

I will never forget that night. I cleaned up my dad and bandaged him and then helped him to bed. I just prayed "God, please help my dad so he will get better. I love him, we all love him."

****

At that point, so much damage had been done. Our family would move on but our lives would never be the same. My dad moved out of the house. My mom really struggled to take care of all the kids. But we never lost faith. Everyone did their best to make things work out. Years later, my dad could proudly say that he was a recovering alcoholic – but there were broken pieces of our family that would never be fixed.

Later in life, I would understand how different my relationship was with my dad (mostly in a good way) compared to the relationship that my other brothers and sisters had with my dad. This has always been very hurtful for me and sad to know that it could have been so different.

As I look back, I can see the effects on all of us kids and realize that mental disorders and severe addictions have a major impact not only on the person who is living with the disorder – but also impact family and friends that are in that person's life.

At this stage of life, I also began to understand more about demons. Demons certainly come in many forms. In the most literal sense, I believe there are evil spirits – Satan and his devils. It is truly a scary thought. We read in the Bible about men and women being possessed by demons. We know that some individuals who exhibited wild, uncontrollable behavior were possessed by evil spirits. Others may have been suffering from mental disorders – which were not at all understood. Many people believed that these individuals were stricken because they had sinned and not repented.

We have certainly become much more educated about mental disorders, but we continue to struggle with the hurtful stigma that exists.

The demons that people face today may even start as a pleasure, but develop into a painful and destructive force: the alcoholic who enjoyed his/her beer or wine or whiskey, then faced a demon who may have destroyed their family, their job, and their health.

For others, they have lived a life as most others – going to school or work, spending time with their friends, raising a family… but then they became sick. Not because they did anything wrong or because they grew up in a bad neighborhood.

It can happen to anyone – no matter how smart, how strong, or how talented they may be. Our brains are all wired in a way to operate properly. But sometimes our wiring becomes faulty and creates major mental problems that can also develop into physical and emotional problems.

Like other body parts, the brain is susceptible to injury and change. This can happen at birth or may not happen until much later in life. Also, some individuals are more predisposed to mental disorders than others.

It is very important to understand your family health history – both mentally and physically. Certainly, in my family, there is a history of mental disorders on both my mom's side and my dad's side of the family.

I strongly urge you to learn about your family's health history and then get educated. There is a lot of helpful information readily available – but also so much more we do not yet understand.

Letter to Dad

Although my Dad has passed away, I still think about him and never want him to be forgotten. I would like to share these thoughts with him.

Dear Dad,

I miss you so much.

I will always remember the good times with you - playing baseball and soccer. You spent many hours teaching me to pitch and I remember seeing how proud you were when you came to see me play my games. I also remember that you constantly encouraged me to be my best and to always be confident. You instilled a strong work ethic in me and lived that out as an example. I remember that you loved God and always went to church with us every Sunday. And I remember that you got up early on weekdays to take me to church when I served as an altar boy. We had great fun rooting for the Cardinals baseball team and loved watching football games on TV. You instilled a spirit of competitiveness in me and taught me to always hang in there when things got difficult. You also taught me to be tough when I needed to defend myself.

You had very little education, but always encouraged me to get a good education and do something great in my life. You were loved by so many people.

And Dad – I forgive you for the hurt that was caused as a result of your drinking problem. I know that you were ill – I just wish that you could have been helped sooner. Mom and the other kids were hurt deeply.

I am thrilled to know that I will see you in heaven. I long to hug you and see you once again.

Love,

Joe

What is happening in our world today?

In July 2015, Hoda Kotb of NBC News reported on Dateline about 'Drunk Drivers.'

The report is very sobering. We are reminded that every night there are people on our nation's roadways, out of control and in possession of a deadly weapon – their car.

Many never get caught so they do it over and over and over. Until one day, they ruin lives.

They are the drunk drivers. We all know that it is bad to drive drunk, and highly dangerous to all of us on the roads. But the worst kind of drunk driver is the repeat offender!

There are millions of them out there putting you in danger every time you drive down the street.

Nothing seems enough to stop these serial drunk drivers – not even arrests, fines, or convictions.

Ms. Kotb shared some unbelievable examples: one man from Iowa had 11 DWI convictions. Another, in New Mexico, has had 14. And in Ohio, there were 18 DWIs for one chronic drunk driver—even though he hasn't had a license in 20 years.

These are just a few examples of the many individuals who continue to drive on our streets and put our lives at risk.

One man says many of these drunk drivers are not just a nuisance or a tragic annoyance with a weakness for alcohol. He has one word to describe a repeat drunk driver who slammed into his world: murderer.

CHAPTER 5

Schizophrenia: My sister – Kathy

> ### *Myth:*
> ### Schizophrenia means that someone has multiple personalities

Kathy was a very pretty little girl. She had a sweet smile, quiet demeanor, and compassionate heart.

She always had a special bond with Billy. There was an unspoken language between the two of them; I think it was a precursor to how we will communicate in heaven. When they hugged, there seemed to be this understanding and love that transcended others. It remains to this very day.

Kathy always loved our family pets – especially our dog Cookie and our cat Fluffy. She was kind to them and they seemed to know how much she really cared about them. Like Billy, she used to share things with the pets – except in her own way. She would take scraps of her food and feed them to Cookie. He would lick her and she would laugh. With our cat, she would pour a little milk from her drink into the cat's bowl. Fluffy would lay in her lap and purr.

Although the youngest of all the children, Kathy was very clever in finding ways to hold her own. As a child, her favorite cereal was Lucky Charms (she loved the multi-color marshmallows; they were the lucky charms). Before anyone got up in the morning, Kathy would sneak in the kitchen and eat as many of the 'lucky charms as possible. One morning, my brother John (who also loved this cereal) sat down to eat his breakfast. He poured a big bowl of cereal and then said with surprise, "where's all the lucky charms?" Kathy was smiling, but didn't tell us she took them until the next day.

****

When things got really bad between my mom and dad, Kathy became very emotionally upset and would not go to school. She told my mom that she wanted to stay home to protect her. The situation got very serious. Truant officers came to the house and had to take Kathy to school. She cried and could not understand why she could not stay home. My mom went to the school to talk to the principal and explain about the situation at home. But the law is the law – Kathy had to go to school.

My mom always felt very protective of Kathy – as well as Billy. I helped my mom a lot with Billy. As he grew older, he became very strong physically and much harder for my mom to control. When I left for college, our family began to split up. Kathy, Janice, and John were very fearful of my dad. I was no longer there to protect them.

When Billy was 18, our family made a difficult decision. Billy was placed in a residential care home which was arranged by a case worker assigned by the state welfare agency. There were very limited choices – but he could not stay at home any longer. My mom had to go to work and start preparing to support herself and my younger brother and sisters.

✶✶✶✶✶✶✶✶✶✶✶✶✶✶✶✶✶✶✶✶

My mom and I went to visit the facility which was recommended by the caseworker. We were shocked. The house was dark and smelled badly. Elderly men and women were left unattended in beds and wheelchairs – many of them moaning and asking for help.

I would not rest until we found a good home for Billy.

My mom and I went to our church to plead for help with the Monsignor. God truly intervened for our family. Billy was placed in a residential care home in Bellefontaine. There were a number of small cottages – separate living quarters for men and women. There were eight residents in each cottage with two full-time attendants around the clock. He even was able to attend a school program during the day to be with other men and women who were at his education level. Our prayers had been answered – at least for now.

Soon after, my mom and dad divorced. My dad would serve as the primary caregiver for Billy. He loved Billy so much and would go to visit him regularly. Without a doubt, it was the most important thing that my dad did for our family. Over the years, my dad would bring Christmas gifts to Billy and the other men in his cottage. Dad would even dress up as a clown and hand out gifts to the residents at their Christmas parties.

****

After several years, my mom remarried and moved to Pennsylvania. Her new husband (Bill) was a very nice man and took very good care of my mom. I was happy for her.

Kathy moved in with my sister Janice and they got an apartment together in Texas. Janice has always been such a good sister and a very loving person. After one year, Kathy and Janice moved to Pennsylvania to be with our mom. It provided some security for them and comfort for my mom.

Both Kathy and Janice started dating and each of them met someone special.

****

Kathy met Tim. He was older than her and worked at the plant with Bill. Kathy felt safe with Tim and moved in with him. They had two children together – a girl and a boy.

One autumn day, when Kathy's children were very young (5 and 3), Tim and Kathy and the children drove to the shopping mall. Tim dropped off Kathy to go shopping and drove off with the kids. He never returned!

Tim had taken off with the kids and went to stay with his mom in Virginia. No one knew where he was for over a week.

Kathy was so distraught that she had a complete breakdown. She was admitted to the local hospital and subsequently put in the psych ward for evaluation.

I received a phone call from my mom. She was crying and screaming at the same time; she was scared for Kathy's well-being and for the safety of her two children. She was angry at Tim but desperate for what to do.

Kathy struggled to get well. Finally, she was released from the hospital and went to live with my mom and Bill. She went for counseling every week and was given medication (lithium) to help her. Kathy was diagnosed with paranoid schizophrenia.

It just seemed unbelievable. How could this happen to my sister? She didn't deserve this – it was so unfair.

We heard from Tim. He said that he could not be with Kathy anymore and that his mom was going to help him take care of the kids. The next two years would be horrible – we would not know how badly until later.

I tried to find out more about schizophrenia so I could help my sister in every way possible. I was stunned at the lack of understanding and how much stigma was associated with mental illness – even by well-educated business professionals.

At work, I was talking with some of my colleagues at lunch. One of my colleagues blurted out, "my boss is really 'schizo' –

just like Jekyll and Hyde." I quickly retorted, "Did you know my sister is schizophrenic?"

Everyone got very quiet... I then added, "Schizophrenia doesn't mean that someone has multiple personalities. It's more common that they may hear voices or think that others want to harm them or don't think rationally. The condition you are describing is related to multiple personality disorder. It's also a mental disorder, but different from schizophrenia."

I realized that education and awareness of mental disorders would be a lifelong challenge.

****

Kathy was in and out of the hospital. She had ongoing problems with hearing voices in her head and thinking that people were looking at her all the time. She was even fearful to walk down the street because she thought that she was being followed all the time.

Sometimes, she would start laughing for no reason at all – it was the voices. From what I have observed, Kathy has been the one in our family to be affected the most by these haughty voices – these strange voices that speak to her. It is scary – and potentially dangerous. If she was to act on what the voices have told her, then she might harm someone – including herself.

On occasion, hearing the voices made Kathy seem like a very different person – shouting out, "what the f*** are you looking at! Get out of here!" All the while, her eyes glared. This was not my sweet sister Kathy. This was some inner demon.

One time, when she was admitted to the hospital after a bad psychotic episode, she had a terrible side effect from one of the medications given to her (Haldol) - strange hallucinations. She was sitting up in her bed and picking the petals off of imaginary flowers - very strange to observe.

It was very challenging for my mom and Bill to have Kathy live with them. Her behavior was often unpredictable, but never harmful – until one summer day.

At the time, they lived in a mobile home. There were certain rules for Kathy about keeping her living area straightened up, not smoking in the trailer, and having a curfew in the evening. Overall, she did pretty well at following the rules.

But one day, a terrible accident happened. Bill was at work, my mom was running errands, and Kathy was home alone. She went outside to smoke some cigarettes. As she tossed one of the cigarette butts, it ignited some trash nearby. Seeing the flames rise, Kathy panicked and ran. The fire spread quickly and totally destroyed the mobile home.

My mom and Bill no longer felt safe to have Kathy living with them.

I told my mom that I would find a place for Kathy to live in Oklahoma (my state of residence at the time) so that I could look after her and visit her. Kathy came to live with me and my family; I felt compelled to do this. Kudos to my family for their love and support in welcoming Kathy into our home.

But there were some scary moments.

I remember waking up at 4 a.m. one night… Kathy was standing next to my bed and watching me. For the first time in my life, I was scared of my sister. I didn't know if she had a knife and would try to stab me or whether she had a bad dream and needed my comfort. I stayed calm and asked her, "Are you okay?" She replied, "Yeah, I'm okay – I just wanted to make sure you were still here." My fear turned to relief and then to compassion for her concern of being abandoned.

Within two months, Kathy was placed in a residential home and I arranged to have her two children placed in a Christian Children's Home in a small town in Oklahoma. As our family looks back, we would have wanted for things to be different – but we did what we thought was best at the time.

****

Initially, Kathy lived in a residential home in Oklahoma. It was not a good experience! I was working in Oklahoma at that time and wanted to place her somewhere that would be within a few hours driving distance. Looking back, I feel like I did what was expedient since it was an urgent situation to get Kathy placed in a home. I wish that I had taken more time and been more diligent. I thank God that He watched over Kathy and kept her from harm.

Our family provided Kathy with clothes and toiletries as well as spending money so she could be part of special activities like going to a show or to go shopping at Walmart. But nothing was safe – any new clothes or money was quickly stolen by other residents. There was no kind of training or daily program to attend and really nothing to do at the home except to watch TV, listen to the radio, or hang out with the other residents. After about one year, I was able to confirm that several of the residents were dangerous and exhibited violent behavior! Kathy told me that she felt threatened and was afraid to live there. At that point, I moved Kathy to a new residential home in Troy, Missouri.

At Troy House, Kathy would be able to attend a state-sponsored daily program with residents from Troy as well as other surrounding residential care homes. The program was hosted at the Headway Club House in Saint Charles, MO. She would be able to participate in support group discussions and would be evaluated quarterly by the program coordinators and counselors. These quarterly reports are sent to me so that I can get updates on how Kathy is doing.

As a resident of Troy House, she also would see medical doctors and a psychiatrist on a regular basis to ensure that she received the proper medications and treatments for both her physical and mental well-being.

✳✳✳✳✳✳✳✳✳✳✳✳✳✳✳✳✳✳✳✳✳✳

I usually call Kathy once per week to check on her and see how she is doing. Sometimes it may be several times per week – depending on whether there is a specific problem or concern that she is dealing with.

There is a range of possibilities of what to expect when I call Kathy. Sometimes when I call, the person answering the phone goes to get Kathy and comes back to tell me that she does not feel like talking or that she has already gone to bed (usually means that she is feeling depressed).

Another possibility is that she will come to the phone and only talk for about 15-20 seconds. The conversation will be something like this.

Kathy: Hello

Joe: Hi Kathy – it's Joe.

Kathy: Oh 'hi'.

Joe: How have you been feeling?

Kathy: I'm okay. I'm really tired. I'll talk to you later.

Joe: I love you Kathy.

Kathy: Thanks for calling – tell your family 'hi'

Joe: Bye Kathy

Occasionally, Kathy will tell me, "I don't' like it here – I want to leave." I feel terrible when I hear that from her. I try to take a deep breath and try to find out what may have happened to make her say that. Usually it's because she has a new roommate or she was told 'no' when she wanted extra coffee or cigarettes. Even so, I know that she probably has those thoughts often. My heart hurts for her.

But there are times when she will come to the phone in a good mood and want to talk and talk and talk... I really look forward to those times. I know that she is doing well and wants to share how she is feeling and wants to know how everyone in the family is doing – especially her two children. It makes it all worthwhile.

Interestingly, Kathy will bring up topics about things that happened over forty years ago. Certain events that happened decades ago seem to be on her mind as if they happened yesterday.

She often tells me, "You know, I think you look a lot like dad." And other times she will tell me, "You know, I think you look a lot like dad – and like mom." In reality, I have certain features that resemble both my mom and dad – but not a strong resemblance. I think that is Kathy's way of having a part of mom and dad that is still with her.

****

Kathy loves coffee and cigarettes. She craves coffee and cigarettes! I know that the caffeine and nicotine are very soothing for her. It is a real struggle to limit her intake. I have talked with the folks at her residential home to ensure that we are aligned about what is best for Kathy – including how much coffee and cigarettes she gets. But this craving for coffee and cigarettes has caused a lot of problems for Kathy.

Just recently, Kathy told me something that was very upsetting. Many years ago, she was desperate to get extra coffee. She talked to one of the men who was at the home. He told her that he would get her more coffee in exchange for letting him touch her.

I was so disturbed by what Kathy told me. It's hard to know if this is the truth. She had just told me that she was not happy at the home and that she wanted to go somewhere else. Something did not seem right. Why was she unhappy all of a sudden? She has been living at this facility for many years. After finding out about the situation with Kathy and "the coffee man", I talked to the Administrator (Diana) at Troy House and she intervened to resolve this problem.

Another incident occurred during this past year, which involved Kathy's craving for cigarettes. I got a call one morning from Diana. I could tell immediately from the tone of her voice that this was serious. She told me that one of the staff members at Troy House reported that she saw Kathy smoking in a restricted area that was banned from smoking by any of the residents. Kathy denied that she was smoking in this area and one of the other residents provided her with an alibi. Keep in mind – this is a 'zero tolerance' offense which would result in Kathy being required to leave the Home! I told Diana that I would talk to Kathy about the situation. Kathy denied smoking in this area and told me that she saw someone else smoking there, but did not know who it was. I did a lot of praying that night and talked to Diana the next morning. Because nothing was conclusive, there was no disciplinary action taken. But it was a frightening experience – I was not prepared to find another Home for Kathy!

I have always been concerned about what really happens to Kathy that I never hear about. I pray for her every day that she will be safe from harm. But I know that it is hard to keep her from harm's way. I want to protect her, but I know there is only so much I can do. Only God can really protect her.

Even though I talk to her and other staff members at the home on a regular basis, I am certain there are many things that I don't know and will never know. Kathy has a pure heart and is very childlike in many ways.

Amazingly, Kathy is very aware of dates and appointments. Once she hears something, she will remember it very well. Unfortunately, she does not always keep things in proper perspective. She tends to treat everything with high priority and a high sense of urgency. She gets very nervous if she thinks there is a problem (especially a medical problem) and it can't be resolved immediately.

That said, Kathy is very resilient. She has endured a lot physically, mentally, and emotionally and has continued to get through it all.

What is happening in our world today?

In March 2015, Eliott C. McLaughlin of CNN reported on a schizophrenic man who was shot by police.

In the report, Mr. McLaughlin tells about Jason Harrison. Jason was at his home in Dallas, standing in the doorway and twiddling a screwdriver between his fingers.

Someone called the Dallas police. When the police arrived, one of the two officers called to Harrison to drop the tool. The officers quickly repeated this command at least four times as Harrison's mom screams, "Jay! Jay! Jay!"

Within 5 seconds of that first command, the 39-year-old schizophrenic man was shot five times, including twice in the back. He fell forward - just a few feet from his mother.

Video from one officer's body camera faded to black as Harrison's mother cried out, "Oh, they killed my son! Oh, they killed my son!" The officers continued to tell Harrison to drop the weapon.

In affidavits, the officers say that they were forced to shoot an armed man who they deemed dangerous after he failed to comply with repeated orders to drop a screwdriver.

As I read about this tragic incident, I thought "How could this have happened? Certainly, these officers should have been trained to handle this situation in a more controlled way. Jason did not have to die!"

CHAPTER 6

Bipolar Disorder: My sister – Mary Ann

Myth:

Bipolar disorder is just another name for mood swings

My sister Mary Ann was the second of six children in our family. As a young girl, she was very slender, quiet, and reserved. During her teen years, she blossomed to be a beautiful girl with long, dark hair, an engaging smile, and great figure. Most people would describe her as very outgoing and very funny!

But Mary Ann lived in a dream world – she was overwhelmed with reality. So often, she would tell our family, and sometimes her friends, outlandish stories; we never really knew what was true because she was always so convincing.

She really found her calling when she joined the drama club in high school. It was really unbelievable. The experience of being on stage and playing some other person was so natural for her. She really gained confidence – she was the star of the show! When our family first saw her perform, we looked at each other and asked in amazement, "is this really our Mary Ann?" Little did we know that her life would always be full of drama.

After Mary Ann graduated from high school, she decided to look for a job; her real desire was to get married and raise a family. Mary Ann was great at interviewing for jobs. She dressed well, had a great smile, and was very friendly. However, once the real work began, she struggled. Something was always a problem: either the people were rude or the work was too hard or she would get sick and not show up. Actually, signs of this problem surfaced when she was very young. As children, we would get paid a small weekly allowance to do chores around the house (clean our rooms, take out the garbage, and the worst of all jobs – clean up the dog poop in the yard!)

Well, Mary Ann really never had any desire to get money. Somehow, she always got what she needed anyway. On the other hand, I was very driven to earn money so I could do things with my friends. So, I always did Mary Ann's chores for her – in addition to mine. She would gladly hand over her allowance to me and we were both happy. We even laughed about it as adults.

Her dream job was to become a travel agent. Somehow, it would allow her to escape the real world and live in a fantasy world. But she would never get her dream job.

****

Mary Ann got married when she was 20 years old. Within four years, she had two children – both boys. She seemed so happy to be a wife and mother.

But this life and all the responsibilities that came along proved to be too much for her. Her total focus was to care for her children as best she could (preparing meals, dressing them, and playing with them). That's about all she could handle.

It was a real struggle for her to clean the house, do dishes, go grocery shopping, and take care of herself. Her husband just did not understand. He thought that Mary Ann was being lazy and just did not care. They began having serious problems in their marriage.

Of course, when we all got together as a family, Mary Ann usually seemed great – put on a big smile, laughed a lot, and had lots of energy. She had some one-liners that were quite memorable. During one of the family meals, her young son Chris asked her if he could have another cookie for dessert. In Mary Ann's unique way of responding, she said, "Sure – it never hurts to have just one more cookie" (that was her personal philosophy on all sweets).

But there was a very different side to her – a side that was severely depressed.

The situation did not get better - Mary Ann got divorced; our family was very sad. Our family did not understand that Mary Ann was sick – mentally sick. Sometimes the people who are closest to someone are the ones who either don't see the problem or just deny that there is a serious problem.

We took Mary Ann to see a psychiatrist – she was diagnosed with bipolar disorder (also called manic depression).

After getting on a regimen of medications, she seemed better for a brief period. She even got remarried. Her second husband was a very quiet man – exact opposite of Mary Ann. They were a good example of the 'opposites attract' rule. But it didn't last long. Mary Ann began having many of the same problems – but this time she was much worse. Her sons lived with their dad and she could not hold down a job.

She did not take care of the house – and she did not take care of herself. Her personal hygiene became a big problem. Her husband did not know how to help Mary Ann – he could not cope with her illness. After three years of marriage, they divorced, Mary Ann moved in with my mom and my Aunt Jan (my mom's sister and best friend).

Mary Ann's behavior was very erratic. In addition to her bipolar illness, she also had other serious health problems – she was very overweight and had extreme blood sugar fluctuations due to her diabetes. She laid on the couch in the family room all day and slept there at night. Mary Ann soiled the couch because she did not care about getting up and taking care of herself. Does not make sense to you and me – but you don't know what it feels like unless you are ill – mentally ill.

My mom and aunt did their best to help her, but it was difficult to care for Mary Ann. The situation was getting very serious.

Mary Ann got very angry with mom for no reason at all. In her head, Mary Ann believed that my Mom was being mean to her. She yelled at my mom and told her, "You don't love me. You don't care about me. I hate you!" In defense, my mom yelled back at Mary Ann and the two of them would get in a terrible yelling match.

Sometimes, Mary Ann would grab my mom and try to hit her. She terrified my mom.

Most of all, my mom was so deeply hurt that her own daughter would treat her so badly. But she kept reminding herself, "Mary Ann is sick. This is not the same sweet daughter that I have loved all my life. She is ill and needs my support and understanding."

****

Our family agreed that Mary Ann needed to be placed in a residential care home. It was best for her and for everyone else. Sometimes it's difficult to admit, but the family does not always do what is needed to set boundaries or enforce certain rules that are in the best interest of someone who is mentally ill.

Mary Ann was placed in a residential care home in Cuba, MO that was about 50 miles away. It was very hard for her to adjust initially – this was a whole new experience. Meals are served at a certain time – if you don't show up on time, then you don't get to eat. You wake up at a certain time so you can get your meds. You get your meds at a certain time each night and then it's 'lights out'. And you also have a roommate which is assigned. You are required to take a shower or bath every day and see the doctor when you are scheduled. Not exactly Mary Ann's style of doing things – but she adapted. It turned out that this routine was actually very good for her.

Overall, it was a nice place for her to live. While helping to find housing for Billy, Kathy, and Mary Ann, I have visited many special care homes – and I have seen some terrible places. There were many reasons – some were very dirty and run down; some had staff who were not qualified or just didn't care; some had residents who were extremely violent or pathetically helpless. Believe me, I would never allow one of my family members to be somewhere that was not safe or had staff that did not care. In this case, I believed that Mary Ann was in a good home.

I also realized that no home, other than your own home, would ever really make you happy. How would you feel? What if you had to go somewhere you didn't want to go – and be with people you didn't know? When you are making a decision about where your loved ones will live, keep that in mind. It is never easy – but can be necessary.

Everyone at the home liked Mary Ann. Most of the time, her behavior was very outgoing. She was very funny and enjoyed the attention. There was also the other side of her – the depressed side. That is the side that was mostly seen by her family. She would cry on the phone and talk about how much she hated being at the home.

Mary Ann never could conquer her love of sweets. For her, this was a life threatening problem. Over time she gained considerable weight. Her blood sugar level would get seriously high on occasion (over 300). She would promise to stay away from sweets, but all too often she would sneak a piece of cake, a few cookies or some chocolates.

She also continued to struggle with her hygiene. It was a real challenge for the caregivers at the residential home to get Mary Ann to take a daily bath or shower. They even tried to compromise with her by agreeing for her to wash up every other day. Sometimes, she would go into the bathroom and run the bath water or shower and tell them that she had cleaned up – only for them to see (and smell) that she had not!

My sister could be very entertaining when she was in her manic state. She would tell wild stories that would be funny and outlandish – but she made them seem so real. She would not filter what she was saying – sometimes it was what everyone else might be thinking, but didn't want to say aloud (reminded me of the movie *Liar, Liar* with Jim Carey).

****

During my research on bipolar disorder, I found a real lack of understanding about this illness. Many people try to oversimplify, but it is actually very complex. There were medications (like Depakote) available to help deal with the symptoms, but there was not a cure. There were many different views about effective treatment plans including individual counseling, group therapy, and even ECT (electroconvulsive therapy).

With ECT, electrodes are placed on the patient's scalp and a finely controlled electric current is applied while the patient is under general anesthesia. The current causes a brief seizure in the brain. ECT is supposed to be one of the fastest ways to relieve symptoms in severely depressed or suicidal patients. It's also considered to be very effective for patients who suffer from mania or other mental illnesses.

But treatment for mental illness is not a 'one size fits all'. Mary Ann was so scared to receive ECT. We talked on the phone many times as I tried to comfort her and help her understand that this treatment might make her feel better. I would always encourage her to "take one day at a time – one step at a time."

It's not easy when your sister, or anyone that you really love, pleads with you and says Help me, please help me - I'm afraid! What would you do? It's a lot easier talking about tough love than to act on it – especially when you are responsible for making decisions on that person's behalf. You just pray that you are doing the right thing for them.

The ECT treatments helped Mary Ann temporarily, but she continued to experience problems – with more depressive episodes than manic episodes.

It is very hard to see someone that you love have to suffer. I saw it with my great grandma. I saw it with Billy. I saw it with my dad. I saw it with Kathy – and now Mary Ann. Why does it have to be our family?

Many people seem sympathetic but don't seem to really understand. I even heard a friend of our family say, "bipolar is just another name for mood swings. They need to be strong and get over it."

I was composed, but very direct when I replied, "bipolar is a brain disorder; it's treatable and can cause a lot of suffering. Individuals can't just snap out of it!"

Letter to Mary Ann

Although my sister Mary Ann has passed away, I still think about her and never want her to be forgotten. I would like to share these thoughts with her.

Dear Mary Ann,

I wish that I could have been with you at the time you passed – it happened so suddenly. But I am thankful for your sake that you passed quickly while you were asleep. God certainly was looking over you and He was ready for you to come home to Him.

We shared a special bond from the time that we were little. As my younger sister, I always tried to watch out for you – but I could not always be there when you needed me. There are times that I wish I would have done more for you.

We had some really fun times together as kids – playing house and playing school. I still remember you and your friends following me around and spying on me when we were in our early teens. And of course, I remember you coming to my fraternity parties – and dating my roommate.

I remember your excitement when you got married and when you had your two children. You were a very loving mom. You were so happy.

But I also remember when you got sick and struggled so much. You were so overwhelmed and so distraught. You tried your best – but it was not enough. No one really knew how sick you were – or what to do to help you. Looking back, everyone wishes that we could have helped you more.

Your life took a turn that would never allow you to return to what we would all call 'normal'. Fortunately, we did find out about your illness – bipolar disorder. And you were able to get help with seeing a psychiatrist and getting medication. But your journey would be a difficult one. Because you had these manic moments which made so many people believe that you were happy and well, it made it harder to understand that you were really ill – since these moments also could be extreme and out of control. And because only those really close to you saw the deep depression you experienced – the sadness and fear and desperation.

But I am so happy that you were able to live in a residential care home and receive good treatment and care. Just prior to your passing, you seemed really happy. You had a boyfriend and everyone at the home really loved you; you were definitely the resident comedian.

I miss your laugh and your hugs. You will forever be in my heart. I know that you will have a big party going to greet me when I get to heaven.

Love you,

Joe

What is happening in our world today?

In December 2012, Richard A. Friedman of the New York Times reported on a mentally ill man who opened fire at an elementary school.

Mr. Friedman tells about a terrible shooting at an elementary school in Newtown, Connecticut and calls attention to the complex links between violence, mental illness and gun control.

The gunman, Adam Lanza, 20, is described as a loner who was intelligent and socially awkward. At the time of the report, no official diagnosis had been made public, but many people were quick to say that keeping guns from getting into the hands of people with mental illness would help solve the problem of gun homicides.

Robert A. Levy, chairman of the Cato Institute, told The New York Times: "To reduce the risk of multi-victim violence, we would be better advised to focus on early detection and treatment of mental illness."

To me, these types of statements are highly misleading. It is true that some individuals with mental illness have committed acts of violence. However, less than 5 percent of violent crimes are committed by individuals with mental disorders, according to the American Psychiatric Association.

****

In addition to the difficulties that Mary Ann was experiencing, the rest of my family was going through their own challenges...

Kathy's two children had been living in a Christian Children's Home for seven years – along with other children whose parents were unable to provide care for them. They were raised by good Christian parents in a loving environment. But it was not their family.

When they were in their early teens (13 and 15), I took guardianship of them and brought them to Houston. It was a huge change for them to come from a very small town in Oklahoma to the big city of Houston. But it would be very important to them later in life.

****

My dad passed away when he was only 62 – had a massive heart attack and died instantly. After the divorce with my mom, he remarried and then divorced after only one year. I knew that he was always in love with my mom.

It was November and very cold in St. Louis when I came in for the funeral. There was a lot of snow on the ground – it reminded me of my days as a child – riding my sled and having snowball fights. I remembered going to Cardinals baseball games with my dad – only three times though. We didn't have much money and he was working a lot.

My dad had a tough life. He grew up in a big family of eight kids, had six kids of his own – but died alone in his apartment.

His twin sister Antoinette and his sister Lorraine were his best friends as he got older. They all looked after each other. I wish things could have been different for my mom and dad – and for us kids.

★★★★★★★★★★★★★★★★★★★

After my dad passed away, my aunt Antoinette took on responsibility for ensuring Billy's welfare – it was my dad's wish. She lived in the St. Louis area and my dad had complete trust that she would make sure Billy was cared for properly. I stay in contact with my aunt to check on Billy and see how he is doing.

When I travel to St. Louis each year, one of my top priorities is to visit with him. I am so thankful for my aunt Antoinette and for her love and care for Billy.

We had real concern when the Bellefontaine Rehabilitation Center (residential home where Billy lives) was in danger of being closed down. Continued funding by the government was in question. There were many old buildings which were in very poor condition and needed to be replaced. The land was in a very desirable location and attracted high interest by developers. We could not believe they would close down this facility. Where would Billy go? He had lived there for over 30 years!

During my visits with Billy, there have been a few times when I noticed that something had happened to him. When he was in his thirties, one of the men in his cottage became violent and severely hit several of the residents – Billy was one of them. He was hit very hard on his right ear. He developed a cauliflower ear (commonly seen with boxers); it would always remain.

In truth, no special care facility is without its' problems – but some definitely more than others. I need to be mindful if I bring other family members with me to go inside the residential facility when we pick Billy up to go out for lunch or come for a family visit. Some of the residents who lived with Billy have demonstrated aggressive behavior, loud yelling, or want to talk to you (fascinating topics: their new girlfriend, their plans to go on a trip, or asking if I can take them home with me).

I try my best to give them some attention because I know that some of them have no one to come visit. I also try to express my appreciation to the caregivers who work in the home – they do not have an easy job. Unfortunately, there is a lot of turnover with these workers – but there are a few who have committed their lives to this work.

But despite many of the challenges, this was Billy's home and he seemed comfortable there. So we prayed that Billy could continue to live at the Bellefontaine home. After months of uncertainty, the facility was given a new start. Funding was provided to make necessary improvements: hire and train new staff, demolish the old buildings and build new ones, and implement new safety and health regulations.

Billy would be able to stay in his home – and it would be even better. A real blessing for Billy and all our family.

****

It was clear to me that many children and adults don't have a good place to live – a place where they will be safe from harm and receive the proper treatment and care needed.

As I explored various agencies and organizations that provide assistance and opportunities for making lives better for mentally retarded individuals, I learned about Special Olympics.

Special Olympics is the world's largest sports organization for children and adults with intellectual disabilities, providing year-round training and competitions to more than 4.4 million athletes in 170 countries. Eunice Kennedy Shriver founded this organization in 1968.

I was so excited to learn about Special Olympics and decided to sign up as a coach for soccer. Even though Billy was not physically able to participate in a sport like soccer, I wanted to help other mentally retarded children and adults in some way.

These folks can't perform at the same level as others who are not disabled. But they possess a determination and a sense of pride and joy that surpasses anything that I have ever observed or felt. Their appreciation is so genuine – their hugs and smiles melt your heart. These folks are truly 'special'. To me, there is no greater Olympic competition in the world.

It's amazing how many other sporting events are part of the competition – including basketball, softball, swimming, table tennis, volleyball, and much, much more.

Whether it's Special Olympics or some other activity, it's very important to provide some type of recreation for all these special individuals who are intellectually disabled.

CHAPTER 7

Anxiety: My mom – Mary Katherine

Myth:

JUST TAKE A PILL AND YOU'LL BE FINE

My mom grew up as the oldest of three children. She had one brother (my uncle Joe) and one sister (my Aunt Jan). Her parents were Joe (the person that I am named after) and Henrietta (always loved that name – the only Henrietta that I have ever known).

Given that my grandparents grew up during the Great Depression, they were always quite frugal. However, my mom told me that they always found a way to do special things for all the kids. My grandpa called my mom "his princess".

From what I was told, my mom was a real tomboy. She would mix it up with any of the boys in the neighborhood – nobody gave her a hard time and got away with it. As she told me, "I would just sock 'em in the nose!"

She always loved sports. Growing up in St. Louis was a great place to live if you liked sports. Over the years, the city has had professional teams in baseball (the Cardinals rule in St. Louis), football, hockey, soccer, and basketball (the Hawks used to be there). So, it was quite natural that my mom would fall in love and marry a good athlete. My mom first got attracted to my dad when she saw him pitching a baseball game.

My mom and dad married when they were both nineteen years old. Because my dad was taking care of his mom at the time, my grandma G. moved in to live with my mom and dad. Now that I have raised a family, I definitely don't recommend having any in-law move in with a newly married couple. But that was more common for their generation.

Within a year, I was born – all 9 lbs. 5 oz. of me (came out as big as most 3 month old babies!) And then Mary Ann was born just sixteen months later. Billy came along twenty months after her. This was just the beginning of a lifetime of caregiving for my mom. She has always been very nurturing – that would be much needed for what was ahead.

Billy, of course, required a lot of special care. But it was different when he was little. He was a child. The challenges would be so much greater as he grew up. Most families would not have more children once they experienced the challenges of caring for a special needs child.

****

Later on, I would find out that's how my dad felt. Being a truck driver on a mediocre salary made it even more difficult to have more kids. But my mom wanted a big family. She convinced my dad that everything would be okay. So after about four years, my brother John was born – and then my sister Janice – and then my sister Kathy.

Of course, a mother loves all her children. But some need more help and care than others. Some would not need that special care until they were older (Mary Ann and Kathy).

I know what it has felt like to be the brother of three siblings with mental disorders. I have taken a lot of responsibility to help care for them and always to protect them. But I could not imagine what it was like for my mom and dad to have three children with mental health problems: Billy – intellectually disabled; Kathy – schizophrenia; and Mary Ann – bipolar disorder.

There are also many different ways that parents dedicate themselves to caring for children with special needs. In this case, these three 'children' needed care for a lifetime. My dad became the primary caregiver for Billy – but it did not require Billy to live with my dad. Billy lived in a residential care facility.

On the other hand, my mom tried her best for Mary Ann and Kathy to live with her at times when they both needed a lot of support and care. But it was too much. Sometimes, the best thing you can do to help your loved ones who are mentally ill is to let go and then be there for them in a different way – to talk on the phone, to visit them, to bring them to your home for the holidays.

As a parent, you never stop being concerned about your kids. I remember well a saying that I heard: a parent is only as happy as their saddest child. There's a lot of truth to that saying. I am so blessed to have three children and two step-children who are all mentally and physically healthy.

Over the years, my mom also became a caregiver for loved ones with physical illnesses. Her second husband (Bill) got cancer and underwent treatments for over a year. My mom was at his side every day. It was a very painful illness. Bill was a large man and it was difficult for my mom to take care of him (bathing, changing clothes, going to the toilet, getting in and out of bed). He died in her arms.

After a few years, she married for the third time (Frank). I got along fine with Frank but I didn't think he was the right person for my mom. He was funny, but very crass. My mom was lonely and wanted companionship. Only after a few years of marriage, history repeated itself. Frank was diagnosed with cancer. He also underwent treatment for an extended time. Once again, my mom was in the role as a full-time caregiver. She was at his side when he passed away.

My mom never complained during all these ordeals. She unselfishly gave herself for her loved ones who needed her. But it all took a toll on her. She became more volatile and more irritable and full of anxiety. She began to have more problems with high blood pressure and headaches. She became much more argumentative and cursed quite a bit.

When my mom talked to her gynecologist, he told her, "just take some pills and you will be fine." As a result, she took large doses of Valium to calm her nerves. But she was not fine.

Her behavior became more erratic over time. Any conversation with my mom was very unpredictable. She lost her ability to filter what she said and quite often she would really shock everyone with her comments. In many cases, it was quite funny. But in other cases, it was quite embarrassing.

Most people have heard the expression 'my nerves are shot' or 'I'm losing it'. I heard this from my mom quite often. Although some people may laugh or give the appearance of joking when saying these words to explain some extreme or bizarre behavior, it's not laughing matter. This may often be a sign that something very serious is going on with that person.

It's quite understandable to me that all the hardships that she faced over many years truly did affect her in a negative way. In fact, our brain is very pliable matter. Just like other parts of our body, we can experience things that make our brain healthy and we can experience things that make our brain ill. We are all wired differently and have a different mental aptitude, toughness, and healing ability. Anxiety (sometimes referred to as panic attacks) can be mild, moderate, or severe. When severe, it can be very debilitating.

Over the years, there have been other examples of severe anxiety in our family. The typical solution has been for a doctor to prescribe some medication - like Prozac. There is no specific age when severe anxiety may occur – it may occur even in very young children.

Almost everyone experiences periods when they feel overwhelmed. But it is not normal to experience extreme fear or panic as a severe chronic condition. This chronic anxiety may manifest in many ways: headaches, sweating, palpitations, and muscle spasms. Eventually, this condition can lead to more serious health problems, including heart disease and stroke.

****

Family members of individuals with mental disorders deal with the situation in many different ways.

As parents, I think there is a natural instinct to protect – you have brought them into the world and raised them. As siblings, I think there is a natural instinct to support and encourage – you have grown up alongside them. As children, there seems to be a wide range of experiences and thinking.

Both Mary Ann and Kathy have always felt a deep love for their children. As mothers, they provided and protected their children – as best they could. In both situations, any semblance of raising their children in a normal home environment only lasted a short time.

Mary Ann's two sons and Kathy's daughter and son have always demonstrated love and concern for their moms. But each of them have struggled with understanding their mom.

Every child, no matter what age, wants to look to their mom as someone who will care for them – not the other way around.

Caring for someone with a mental disorder is always difficult. All facets of our being are affected – mental, physical, emotional, and spiritual.

Mentally – there is a need to understand and become educated about the disorder. Usually, the more someone understands, the more willing and able they will be to help.

Physically – there is a need to touch. Holding hands, hugging, maybe even a kiss. We all need affection. Often, we don't know how to show affection.

Emotionally – there is a need to empathize and sometimes sympathize. Connecting with someone emotionally can be confusing and frustrating, but also rewarding and fulfilling. I believe that emotional connection can be the most powerful way of showing support, love, and concern. It's important to know that the emotions of individuals with a mental disorder can be very erratic and irrational – not because they are trying to be difficult – but because they are ill.

Spiritually – there is great power. There comes a time of realization for almost everyone that some challenges are beyond our own capability to resolve. But not always a willingness to admit it or a desire to turn things over. Been there, done that. However, it's not about your needs or doing things your way. It should be about seeking help in every way possible for that person you know with a mental disorder. There's no greater power than God.

For all the caregivers of the world, there will be sacrifice and disappointment and hurt – but there can also be fulfillment and joy. I am so thankful for my mom and all those like her who are willing to sacrifice for the welfare of others.

CHAPTER 8

Caregivers:
Pile On Effect

> *Myth:*
>
> **IF YOU ARE A STRONG PERSON, YOU WILL NOT
> EXPERIENCE MENTAL HEALTH PROBLEMS**

My work schedule became quite hectic. I was VP Human Resources and there were a lot of very long work days. The combination of work and family issues was taking a toll. I went to see my doctor and he scheduled a stress test for me.

On the morning of the test, I arrived at the hospital. Just prior to starting my test, I got a phone call from my brother John (he never calls me early in the morning). My sister Mary Ann had passed away during the night; she went into diabetic shock and never recovered. She was only 56 years old. She died peacefully.

You always hear that no parent should have to bury their children. None of us saw this coming – and it hit our family hard. But most of all, my mom. After hearing the news, my wife Lea and I immediately got on a plane to St. Louis.

I made arrangements for Mary Ann at the funeral parlor. My sister Janice flew in from Pennsylvania; my brother John and my sister Kathy were already in the St. Louis area. Billy would not be able to attend – it would be too upsetting for him.

When we first told Kathy about Mary Ann passing away, she was in disbelief. She kept asking, "is she really dead – are you sure?" My mom was in shock – she was very thankful to have all of us with her to provide comfort.

The funeral service was very simple. Mary Ann was laid out in a casket that was rented; she was going to be cremated. That was my mom's decision. Mary Ann actually looked happy – the way we wanted to remember her. She also looked at peace – what we have always wanted for her since she became mentally ill.

There were about twenty people at the service – family members and a few close friends. Mary Ann's first husband, Noel, attended. He told our family that he was really sorry about Mary Ann passing away – and that he wished he would have known she was really sick (mentally ill) when they were married. He would have tried to help her more.

Mary Ann's two sons also attended. I know they loved their mom very much – but also struggled with how to understand her. I see the situation with Kathy and her two children to be very similar.

I led the service and delivered the eulogy – recalling some of the things that happened when we were growing up (the good memories). Also offered an opportunity for anyone to share their thoughts about Mary Ann. Well, there were some great stories told about her – most of them very amusing! Mary Ann definitely had a way of making people laugh!

****

Less than a year after Mary Ann died, my mom had chest pains and was admitted to the hospital. You need to understand that there might have been lots of reasons why my mom had chest pains. Whatever she did, she went all out. She loved playing with her kids and with her grandkids and nephews and nieces.

One time I called her to see how she was doing (she was 74 at that time). She was watching her grandson (Ryan – he was 10 at that time). I could tell there was a lot of noise in the background and asked what's going on mom? She responded with excitement, "Oh, Ryan and I are playing hockey in the basement – I'm the goalie." That's my mom.

****

Back to the hospital...

It was December and extremely cold in St. Louis with about six inches of snow on the ground. Many people were getting sick and the flu was rampant. Seemed very natural that my mom might be having some problems with so many people getting ill – especially the elderly (she was now 79 years old).

My wife Lea and I made a trip to St. Louis to be with my mom. My aunt Jan was there with her also. They ran some tests and gave her meds – she seemed to be doing better and was sent home. We were all very hopeful that she would continue to get better and be able to enjoy the holidays.

Two weeks later she was back in the hospital. Same problem – chest pains. Lea and I made another trip to be with her. My brother John also came to the hospital to see mom. Really tough for him to come - he was disabled due to a very serious work accident fifteen years ago.

After two more weeks in the hospital, my mom's condition became much worse. My aunt told me that the situation was serious. Once more, Lea and I made a trip to St. Louis to be with my mom at the hospital. After doing biopsies on her lungs, she was diagnosed with viral pneumonia. She was put on a ventilator – she could not breathe on her own.

By the next day, the doctors told us that there was nothing else they could do for my mom. I had to face the reality that my mom would not recover. I sat by her bedside and read to her the book of Psalm from the Bible. I was not sure what she could hear – but I wanted to surround her with praise and thankfulness.

While resting in my mom's hospital room, nothing else in the world seemed important. It was all about being in the moment. I held her hand and talked to her – telling her how much all her family loved her and thanking her for all she had done for us.

The nurse then disconnected the ventilator – and she breathed her last breath.

Letter to Mom

Although my Mom has passed away, I still think about her and never want her to be forgotten. I would like to share these thoughts with her.

Dear Mom,

As your oldest child, I have always felt a special bond with you. You confided in me about your happiest moments as well as your saddest moments. You instilled in me a loving, caring, compassionate spirit. You have lived a life of unconditional love and sacrifice.

Throughout my life, you have always been my biggest fan. No matter what happened – you always praised me and encouraged me. What a wonderful gift you have given me by making me feel good about myself. I wish that more parents could do this for their children. You also loved each of your six children with all your heart – we all could see that and feel that love.

I remember you playing with us when we were young; this carried on with your grandkids. You had amazing energy and enthusiasm. You certainly fit the expression 'forever young'. Your happiest times were with young children – whether your own kids or grandkids or nieces and nephews. Until I became an adult, I could not fully understand or appreciate your role as a mother of several children with special needs – Billy, Kathy, and Mary Ann. I also have realized that you never stop being concerned and feeling responsible for your children – no matter what their age.

I also realize how these challenges took their toll on you. You would always try to be so strong for everyone else – yet you needed help too. Your pain and anguish had to be masked with medication – yet you continued to be there and care for your family. I am glad that you shared your feelings with me – the good and the bad. It was difficult living away from you since the time that I graduated from college. I remember, during the later years of your life, how you wished for me to move closer so we could see each other more often.

I am thankful that I could be at your side, holding your hand, during your last moments here on earth. I am thankful and feel very blessed that you are my mom. I miss you so much. But I rejoice in knowing that I will reunite with you in heaven. I know that you will greet me with your hugs and kisses – as you have done your whole life.

I love you,

Joe

****

I have heard people say, "If you're a strong enough person then you won't have mental problems." That is so wrong! It is a fact that mental disorders can affect anyone – regardless of their age, race, wealth, intelligence, or physical prowess.

In so many ways, my mom was a very strong person. I am amazed how she was always there to support, encourage, and care for others. The challenges that she faced during her lifetime were truly overwhelming.

I saw my mom at her best and I saw her at her worst. But through it all, I saw her as a loving, caring, compassionate woman.

CHAPTER 9

ALZHEIMER'S: MY UNCLE – JOE

> ## *Myth:*
> ## IF SOMEONE IN YOUR FAMILY HAS DEMENTIA, THEN YOU WILL HAVE IT TOO

My uncle Joe was named after his dad (my grandpa). Joe is a family name – my grandpa, my uncle, my great uncle, my uncle's son, and me.

Uncle Joe was fairly tall for his generation at 6'3" and very slender. He has a pet poodle – he loves that dog. Takes her on a walk every day; actually several times a day if possible. His favorite pastime is to watch golf on TV.

As kids, we affectionately called my uncle 'Superman'; we still do to this day. I still remember him lifting me up when I was little and thinking he was so strong.

Uncle Joe was also very artistic. He used to make sculptures from bars of soap (Snoopy dog, fox, fish); very awesome.

When my uncle was 30, he bought a brand new, red Mustang convertible. Wow – I thought this was the coolest car on the road. He was so proud of that car.

My uncle spent a lot of time on the road. He spent many years selling farm equipment and arranging for financing for the equipment. It required him to cover the Midwest territory and travel to a lot of small towns. But he liked it – this work suited him well.

✶✶✶✶✶✶✶✶✶✶✶✶✶✶✶✶✶✶✶✶✶✶

Amazingly, my uncle has stayed very fit through the years   He likes to ride his bicycle and take walks; he has never been a big eater.

He continued to work until he was 70. My uncle looked forward to his retirement years with much enthusiasm.

About the time that he turned 75, he experienced some health problems and had a heart attack. He recovered very well and was highly committed to taking good care of himself.

But then a new problem started.

✶✶✶✶✶✶✶✶✶✶✶✶✶✶✶✶✶✶✶✶

Gradually, my uncle began to be very forgetful. It started to be very erratic (off and on) but then began to be happening most of the time. My aunt Rose (my uncle's wife) was still working a full-time job. Mostly to keep good medical benefits for them.

She loved my uncle very much, but it became increasingly difficult for her to take care of him.

His condition declined pretty rapidly. It was clear that my aunt Rose would need to be home with him; she retired from her work in order to be at home with my uncle.

It was very difficult for all our family to see each other. My Uncle Joe and Aunt Rose lived in a small town in Iowa. My family and I live in Houston. My Aunt Jan, my brother John, my brother Billy, and my sister Kathy all live in the St. Louis area. As a result, I have not been able to see my uncle very often and observe how his condition was declining.

He could not go out of the house by himself; he would not be able to find his way home. And he also got confused about names. Sometimes he would remember the relationship (that's my wife or that's my daughter); but he could not recall their name.

The doctors diagnosed his condition as Alzheimer's. He was given medicine (Namenda XR) to help slow the process.

✳✳✳✳✳✳✳✳✳✳✳✳✳✳✳✳✳✳✳✳✳✳✳✳

Last year, my aunt Rose developed lung cancer. She went through radiation and chemotherapy treatments. Initially, she showed some progress and her tumor shrank. Over time, the tumor grew again and she had to resume treatment. During this time, my aunt Jan (my uncle's sister) went to stay with my uncle Joe and Aunt Rose to help them. My aunt Jan is one of the most caring and selfless people that I know.

Then, something truly unexpected happened – my Aunt Rose had a stroke and passed away.

It was so difficult for my uncle to understand. For the entire first week after his wife passed away, my Uncle Joe would wake up in the morning and ask, "Where is Rose?" My aunt Jan would need to tell him that she passed away – and he would weep. He had to relive this day after day.

A few months later, my uncle had his 80th birthday. We all made plans to meet in St. Louis for a celebration and family reunion.

It was so great to see my uncle. But it was also hard to see him – he was not the same man. He greeted us and smiled – then said, "Now, who are you?" I just thought, "how could this happen? This is Superman!"

Just 2 minutes after we told him, he would ask again.

As my uncle sat on the couch, his poodle lay at his side while he gently stroked her back over and over and over. He told us very happily, "you know, every day, we (the dog and him) take a walk around the block. When we get home, she lays by my side and I pet her just like this."

I am not exaggerating – he repeated that same story about 20 times in one evening and told it with great pride every time.

****

During my visit to St. Louis, I also spent time with Kathy, Billy, and John.

It was just a few years ago when Kathy had experienced severe pain and underwent tests to detect the problem; it was uterine cancer. She was very upset and concerned that she might die. Kathy had an operation which was very successful. We were all so thankful and Kathy was very relieved.

Billy looked great. It made me so happy to see him. He was in good shape physically and seemed very calm emotionally. During our time together, we took a moment to touch our foreheads together – our special sign of love for each other.

John made an extraordinary effort to get together with the family four nights in a row – very tough for him to do! He is in constant pain due to severe injuries to his neck, back, and feet (all crushed in an accident at work). He needs to get regular treatments and requires very strong pain medication. He is amazing – remains positive in spite of tremendous pain every day.

My brother John is my hero. I can't imagine the pain that he endures every day. He has shared with me the pain, the depression, and the desperation that he feels. He continues to be strong – taking one day at a time. There no longer seems to be any operation or any medication that will make a difference in helping him. He has endured numerous concussions from falling, numerous blood clots from injuries and operations, and he keeps going. But I can hear in his voice that he is hurting –

physically, mentally, and emotionally. I just know that he will have his peace and comfort one day when he gets to heaven.

****

After my uncle Joe and his daughter (Kris) went back home to Iowa, Kris began to look at options for providing care for my uncle. Kris is a school teacher and would need help.

She arranged for several people to come by the town house to meet my uncle and see who might be a caregiver for him on a part-time basis. Well, when Kris talked to my uncle and asked, "How did you like that person?" My uncle would respond and say, "Oh, they seemed nice."

Then Kris would say, "How would you like for them to come by and have lunch with you each day and just check to make sure everything is okay?"

Well, that did not go over well at all with my uncle. His response was, "I don't need anybody to babysit me!"

After talking with my uncle further, he has agreed for someone to come by for a couple hours each day to have lunch with him.

However, this was not going to be enough. Kris knew that her dad needed someone to be with him more than just a couple hours each day. What could she do? She was not ready to put him in a home – and he certainly would be very resistant if she tried.

So she decided that she would move in with him. She would continue to work full-time at her teaching job, but she could be with my uncle Joe during the evenings, early mornings, weekends, and all summer. Not an easy choice – but the best option for now.

Kris put her house up for sale – there was no way she could keep up her own home plus her dad's townhome. What about her own social life? What if her dad got worse and she could not take proper care of him? The 'what if's' seemed endless.

After moving in with her dad, it did not take long before the stark reality hit Kris – this is really hard! What a huge responsibility to take on – but it was her choice. We all have a choice. We can give lip service and say we really care or we can put our words into action.

Kris has made a very loving and very courageous choice. But these difficult choices can take a toll on you. I think it was captured well when Kris recently made the comment, "I don't feel like I have a life anymore!"

It's easy for any family caregiver to feel that way. In fact, it would be rare not to feel overwhelmed at times. And not only do caregivers have challenges at home, but also with others – friends, co-workers, even other family members.

Over the last few months, my uncle has experienced several episodes that were very troubling.

One morning, for no apparent reason, he said, "Jesus told me that I will be going to heaven soon."

Two days later, he said, "I killed myself this morning; really I did!" Then, one minute later, he seemed very confused and whispered, "why did I say that?" What prompted this obsession with death? No one knows.

My uncle Joe wanted to do things the right way – he just was not sure how. Knowing how to do even little things – like taking his pills - could become very frustrating and really upset him. Have you ever tried to take pills by picking them up with a fork? My uncle did. What if you were told to chew your pills one day because they were something 'extra' you needed to take and they wanted you to chew (instead of swallowing) all your other pills? Seems confusing to me. What if you were told to take your pills with water and then dumped your pills into the glass of water so you could do as instructed! I actually thought that showed some real creativity on his part.

He also has experienced paranoia and delusions. Kris has found him in the bathroom during the middle of the night in total darkness; he was hiding because he was convinced that someone was trying to hurt him. Definitely all warning signs that his condition was getting worse.

It was time to do something different to provide the proper care for my uncle. But what is the right thing to do? A next step may be to find a day care program so that he would receive care and supervision all day long while Kris was teaching; she could still be with him in the evenings and on weekends. Another option would be to place my uncle in a nursing home, which provided special care for his needs. It was not an option for Kris to quit teaching and devote full time to caring for her dad. She loves him so much – but just wants to do what is best for him. Given my uncle's current condition, Kris is now making provisions for my uncle to attend a day program. She will take him in the morning and pick him up in the afternoon when she gets out of school.

****

It is quite possible that his condition will get worse. Like you, I'm sure that you have seen movies or read articles or may even know someone personally affected by Alzheimer's. I am overwhelmed with sadness when I see family members that care for loved ones who are sick and may not even be recognized – as their spouse or as their child. I can't imagine how that would feel, yet I know that time may come. Even worse, I may be the one who becomes sick and needs care.

How much patience would you have if you needed to care for a family member who could not remember your name – or could not remember what you did to help them fifteen minutes ago? Sometimes this can also involve physically demanding tasks like giving a bath or shower, wiping them after they go to the toilet, turning them over in bed so they don't get sores – and the list goes on.

I don't think any of us know how you would deal with this kind of situation until it happens. But don't try to do it alone. Seek help - no matter how much you love someone or how strong of a person you are.

And be prepared that many people, even good friends, may say or do things that are upsetting because they just don't understand – so many people are misinformed.

One of Kris' friends told her, "I heard that if someone in your family has dementia, then you will definitely have it too."

Kris replied, "that's not so – some forms of dementia do have a genetic component, but it's not definite that it will be passed on."

We need more research, more education, more treatments, more cures.

What is happening in our world today?

During August 2015, Arnie Schaenzer of the Liberty Patch (IL) newspaper reported on an elderly woman with Alzheimer's who was missing.

The 77-year-old woman suffered from Alzheimer's. When she was reported as missing, police believed that she could be in danger.

The woman, Mitsuko "Mikko" Washinush, was reported missing from her home in the 1800 block of White Fence Lane in Green Oaks on Monday, according to a Lake County Sheriff's

Office press release. Her family members last saw her around 8:30 a.m. that morning.

"Her family left for a morning appointment and when they returned at approximately noon, she was no longer home," according to the news release. "It's believed she left on foot and became confused, forgetting her way home".

Ms. Washinush suffered from other medical conditions in addition to Alzheimer's.

****

I'm not sure if this woman was found. When I read this report, I thought about my uncle and how concerned I would feel if he was missing. Unfortunately, this is a very common problem for individuals with Alzheimer's.

CHAPTER 10

DEPRESSION: MY STORY

> *Myth:*
>
> **IF YOU CAN'T GET OVER DEPRESSION,
> THEN YOU DON'T HAVE ENOUGH FAITH**

I spent many years of my life trying to be a perfectionist (definitely has its upside and downside). Finally realized that this is not a very practical way to live. Bottom line: whatever you do or what others do will never seem to be good enough.

My mom told me that when I was only 5 years old, I would go around the house and 'straighten' things. If a knickknack was slightly out of place, I would make sure it was moved where it should be. If a picture was crooked, I would adjust it (you get the idea – I was a neat freak).

I have always loved going to school. In fact, when I was in kindergarten (only went half days), I asked my mom if I could go to both class sessions – morning and afternoon. She talked to my teacher (Mrs. Geitz) and she said, "Well, I have never had a student ask to do this, but I am glad to give it a try."

I was so excited. So, the next day I went to my morning session and then went home to eat lunch. When I returned for the afternoon session, it was all different kids (of course)! I was devastated. I walked into the coat closet and asked my teacher to call my mom and take me home. Still laugh about this incident to this day.

****

Growing up, I was always a very good student. Made excellent grades – but I had to study hard. But this was a way for me to excel; in school, your academic accomplishments are very measurable – grades. It was very important to me to make excellent grades.

I had a goal of being the first one in either my mom or dad's family to graduate from college. I had a plan and I would work hard to make it happen. My dad always instilled a strong work ethic in me – this would be a real strength for me throughout my life. It's about going above and beyond – it's about keeping on when others are ready to give up.

At 15, I got my first real job. I worked part-time in the stock room in a very nice jewelry store (my dad delivered packages to this store and got me the job). It was a great job for a high school kid.

I attended McBride high school in St. Louis. This was one of the best high schools in the area. It was a magnet school which attracted strong academic talent from all over the city.

McBride was an all-boys school; similarly there were a few all-girls schools in the city.

I received an excellent education at McBride and made some great friends (want to give a shout out to Rick H, John M, Kevin P, Gerry K, Mike C, Mike N, Bob K., Jim O, Larry G., and John D). But with no girls, it lacked a lot of social perks. Most likely, I was a lot more focused on my classes than I would have been otherwise.

During the summer after my junior year, I worked for my uncle Mike doing concrete construction. More than any other job I have done, this one truly motivated me to get my college education. This was tough work! My uncle was a hard-nosed boss. In the concrete construction business, I worked alongside some real characters (got a real education on life that summer). Must say that this job really helped to build me up physically – great workout every day.

Sports have always been a big part of my life. During high school, I ran track and played football. Without a doubt, one of the most awesome experiences of my life was playing football during my senior year.

Our high school had the smallest number of students compared to all the other schools in our conference. But we were a school with great pride and a drive to win. I will never forget the two-a-day workouts during the summer before the season started – they were brutal.

Because we were a small school, we had a few players (including me) that played both offense and defense. That year, our team went 9-1 and won the conference championship. We were one of the top ranked teams in the state and enjoyed celebrity status at school. You know the old saying about everyone having 15 minutes of fame (well, this was one of those moments).

There was one moment I would like to forget. During our first game of the season, I made an open field tackle running full speed on a punt and had a head to head collision with the ball carrier. It was a great tackle – but we both went down hard. My mom was in the stands and tried to come on the field to make sure I was okay (fortunately my dad stopped her). Love you mom.

During my senior year, I applied to several colleges and decided to attend the University of Missouri at Rolla – now known as Missouri University of Science and Technology. I received a partial academic scholarship and was accepted into the Co-Op program with McDonnell Douglas in St. Louis which would allow me to pay my own way through college. I chose Computer Science as my major – turned out to be a great decision for my career.

****

At this time, my life was bittersweet. I had such a wonderful experience in high school. Got a great education and made honor roll every term. Played sports, won a football championship, and made some amazing friends. Awarded a scholarship for college along with an internship. Even started dating a really great girl.

But life at home with my family was difficult. The situation with my mom and dad was getting worse, my brothers and sisters had depended on me to be there and help protect them, but I was getting ready to leave home for college. Billy was getting hard for my mom to handle; Kathy was struggling to go to school; Mary Ann spent a lot of time talking on the phone and bumming around with her friends – and crying in her room.

I have always tried to be a person of strong faith. My faith has definitely been put to the test many times. I have been knocked down more than a few times. But I have always gotten back up and come back stronger. I think about these times as 'moments of truth'.

These moments define who you are as a person – they build character and define what you stand for. Upon starting college, many beliefs that you have been raised with are challenged. I think it is important to really understand why you believe what you believe so that you embrace those beliefs as your own – and not just what was told to you.

I remember one of those 'ah ha' moments. While in college, I was learning so much and I became painfully aware how much I didn't know. It also became a time when I was like a big sponge and wanted to soak in all the knowledge that I could. This included becoming more educated about mental disorders.

Initially, I was focused on understanding more about mental retardation to know how to help Billy. But I also wanted to understand more about dysfunctional families and some of the effects on parents and children – including alcoholism and depression. I also began to understand about the concept of predisposition (inclination or susceptibility to being affected by a certain disorder or disease). Also learned about genetic and environmental factors which can be significant factors in the onset of mental disorders. I never realized that this education would be a lifelong endeavor.

****

My college years were very pivotal years for me. It was a time for me to be away from home for the first time and just focus on me. Sounds a bit selfish, but I needed a break from all the drama that I had been dealing with at home.

My freshman year at college was awesome. I joined a fraternity (Sigma Tau Gamma) and was voted to be President of my pledge class. The Sig Tau's were a great group of guys. My experience during freshman year was a bit like the movie 'Animal House'. I did really well on my grades during the first semester (required in order to get admitted to the frat) and then went a bit wild during my second semester. Seemed like I had a lot of pent up anxiety that needed to be released.

I made a lot of good friends that year. Want to give a big shout out to Charlie K. (my first roommate), Bob K. (probably the most sensible guy in our class), 'Cotton' (a true rival to Robert Redford), Bob R. (super smart), Sal P. (one of the nicest guys you could ever meet), 'Zapper'(honored to have him as VP responsible for our pledge class), 'Beeps'(missed his calling as a stand-up comedian), "Popper"(who helped get me through my first Computer Science class), Ron M. (a born leader), Joe W. (probably the craziest guy I ever met – except for his younger brother Tony), and the list goes on...

During my sophomore year, I was on a semester break from school for my intern assignment. Made a big decision to get married and take a semester off school. Had two character building jobs – selling encyclopedias door-to-door (people used to actually do that) and working as a superintendent of sales and service in a very large cafeteria. Both jobs totally motivated me to get back in school as soon as possible.

I graduated with my B.S. in Computer Science and moved to Houston to take my first job with Conoco. By the time I was 26, I had three kids – a daughter and two sons. I loved these years when my kids were young during my 20s and 30s. Had such a great time teaching them to ride a bike, helping them with their homework, playing in the backyard, and coaching them in sports.

It was hard living away from my family in St. Louis. I did my best to stay connected with my mom and my brothers and sisters. After my mom and dad divorced when I was 20, I did not hear from my dad as frequently. He did come visit me in

Houston the year before he passed away; we went to a baseball game at the Astrodome to see the Cardinals play the Astros (I still have the baseball cap that he wore that day).

****

I don't remember experiencing severe depression until I was in my early 40's. All my life, I was so strong for everybody else. For my mom, for my dad, for Billy, for Kathy, for Mary Ann, for my kids. Now it was me – I had to be strong for me.

For many years, I had a lot of ways to be fulfilled. I was blessed with 3 healthy, beautiful children. I was a deacon and Bible class teacher. I was making great progress in my career –and led campaigns for United Way and participated in Special Olympics events in Houston. I continued to play soccer on club teams until my late 30s.

How could someone with all these blessings ever get depressed? It can happen.

Although there were all these wonderful things happening in my life, I always had a void. As a man, I tend to compartmentalize everything. Everything and everyone in my life fits in a certain box in my mind. I keep these boxes very organized – but also very separate. Each box can be opened and closed when needed. For me, it is the way to cope with so many demands and so many things that are painful.

I have boxes for my spiritual being: first and foremost – God. My vision is to go to heaven – nothing is more important! I do believe in Jesus as my Savior and that He died to save me. What an awesome and wonderful gift. My mission is to bring glory to God while I am here on earth – to love God with all my heart, soul, mind, and strength. Because of my faith, I have submitted myself in baptism and I am committed to worship and serve my Lord. So, my spiritual life is manifested through prayer, worship, giving, study, teaching, and serving others.

But there was conflict.

I have a 'thorn' that tortures me. We all have things that cause us pain. Some are here for a short time, some come and go, and some never seem to go away. So, why don't we just pluck the thorn and burn it? Because sometimes the thorn brings us pleasure and we have a hard time letting it go. But how can that happen? Usually, it happens gradually – starts small and grows and grows. Before you know, you desire this thorn. This thorn may be an addiction: alcohol or drugs or sex; this thorn may be power or money or position; this thorn may be possessions or appearance. What is your thorn?

What happens when we live with these thorns? For me, there is turmoil inside. Because there is a battle going on between what I believe is right and what I seek and think about. So, I try to put it in a separate box and contain it. Then, all my other boxes will be okay. Guess what – that doesn't work! So, I began to feel bad about myself. The more my thorn got deeper and deeper, the more I felt guilty. Then I would feel sorrow. I would close the box on my thorn and feel better again. I felt guilty and I felt sorrow, but I did not truly turn away from my thorn. I wanted to change – but… We all have excuses. We all can find ways to rationalize what we think and do. We may blame it on our upbringing or family history. It is true that many folks are predisposed to certain illnesses or disorders. That certainly seemed to apply to me. But I knew that was not the answer.

And I began to feel very depressed…

I also have boxes for my mental being. My vision: serve in a senior leadership role for a major corporation. I am not overly ambitious – such as being CEO of General Electric or Chairman of IBM. But I always believed that I have a natural ability to lead others. During any career, there are certain times which will be available to match your interests and abilities with opportunities that come your way. In many ways, the quality of your life is very dependent on your ability to make good decisions at these key times.

For me, one of these key times occurred when I was working at Conoco. I was working on a very strategic IT project, which had potential for changing work processes on a global basis. These are the kind of projects that you relish to work on during your career. After initial work was completed on cost/benefit analyses, the company decided to form a global project team to be based in the U.K. and comprised of key functional leaders from seven countries. I was asked to lead the U.S. team and go on an expatriate assignment. Wow! What an awesome opportunity.

But there was a conflict.

As the saying goes – be careful what you wish for. Really? Yes – really. It's a matter of keeping priorities straight. This assignment would offer some amazing opportunities to travel throughout Europe and visit with the subsidiary offices in countries like Norway, Ireland, Belgium, Germany, and Scotland as well as live in Stratford-upon-Avon (where Shakespeare grew up) and experience all the wonderful sights in London.

However, at this time, my youngest son, Jason, was a junior in high school and I did not want to move him to the U.K. during his junior / senior years. My other two children, Amy and Mike, were already in college. But it was important for Jason to finish his high school education in the U.S. So, I went on the expat assignment alone. My family would be able to join me during the summertime when school was not in session. This was such an amazing career opportunity – just had to make it work! This would be the first time that I would be away from my family for an extended period of time. But they were all supportive for me to go.

The work assignment was phenomenal. Great experience and great exposure to company executives. But my thorn pricked me – hard. The pain was deep – very deep. My support system was gone – my family, my church, and my close friends. But I would work through it. I always work through it. I am resilient, persistent, and hard-working. So I did.

My family needed me – but I was not there for them. I needed to complete this assignment and then everything would be good. I was trying my best to handle everything. I remember one day while I was standing in the shower; I fell to my knees and wept and cried out to God, "please help me, Father; I need you; show me the way."

And I felt very depressed...

I have boxes for my physical being. My vision: to stay in good shape, maintain a nice appearance, and remain healthy. I have always been active and loved to play sports; that has allowed me to feel good and look good. For many years, I maintained a workout program – running, aerobics, and walking as well as playing soccer and softball. In addition, I take my daily vitamins and minerals. I love all kinds of food – definitely one of life's great pleasures. But usually, I eat pretty healthy (my weakness is chocolate). During my expat assignment in the UK, I was exposed to many different cultures during my travels to many European countries. It was very exciting to experience the taste of new foods and drinks, the sound of new music, the view of new scenery, and developing new relationships with people who talked differently and lived differently.

But there was conflict.

My thorn was back. I tried to be strong. I was doing so well. But the thorn pierced me – deeper and deeper and deeper – until I began to change in a way that troubled me. I could tell that my friends around me could notice – something is different about

Joe; something is wrong. I lost my ability to set boundaries. I found myself trying to be all things to all people. It doesn't work very well. For most people, including me, the result is burnout. Trust me, you don't want to go there. Burnout will affect all aspects of your life and can be very damaging. I was not sleeping well. I was losing weight and feeling very fatigued. I was having bad headaches. I was not exercising. I was not eating properly. I literally felt sick to my stomach – every day.

And I felt very depressed…

I also have boxes for my social / emotional being. My vision: to be a loving husband and father, and to be an honorable friend to those at church, work, and the community. I was blessed to grow up with two brothers and three sisters; we have always shared a close bond and a genuine love for each other. Because of all the special needs of our family, there has been a high level of care and dependence among us. Then I was blessed with three children of my own. When my children were growing up, I experienced some of the greatest joys of my life. We all went to church together and participated in youth group activities. I helped each of my kids with school projects and homework – each with their own needs (going through Algebra and Geometry three more times was actually fun for me since I have a minor in Math). I also coached both Mike and Jason in sports – primarily soccer and baseball. Both of them were outstanding soccer players and we traveled to other cities frequently to compete in premier leagues and tournaments. Amy participated in chorale and was an outstanding student.

She was very involved with the youth group at church – also one of my great joys. I have always been so proud of my children.

At church, I made some great friends. Many of these folks were truly like family – especially because my parents and siblings were remote. At work, I was known by many as 'smiling Joe' because I had a very happy demeanor and got along well with everyone.

But there was conflict.

I felt confused. I felt anguish. There was a war going on inside me - my sword of truth vs. my thorn. The war continued and I became weary. My family and friends rallied behind me to support me and I won a huge battle! I was at peace; it would all be okay. But my thorn was not removed – only hiding. Then it struck again – and with a vengeance.

Gradually, some of my family pulled away from me. Many of my church friends turned their backs on me. I found out who would stand by me when things got really difficult. You may be surprised who will stand by you and who will not. But I know that many who turned their backs on me just did not understand what I was going through. Maybe someday…

But at that time, I felt very depressed…

I found myself rationalizing certain actions by just opening and closing boxes as needed. I would shut out the things that parts of my brain that caused conflict with other parts of my brain. It was as if they did not exist. It depended on the situation based on my circumstances – being at church or work or home or with friends. It was not even intentional – I changed and adapted depending on what the situation called for. I felt like a human chameleon. But this caused a lot of internal conflict and much pain, sadness, guilt, and loneliness.

✶✶✶✶✶✶✶✶✶✶✶✶✶✶✶✶✶✶✶✶✶✶✶✶✶✶✶✶

I am glad to tell you that I did get help; met with several psychiatrists and psychologists over a five year period, took medication (Effient helped the most), and did a lot of praying.

There are some other things that are important. You need to surround yourself with a support system – both family and friends. This is easier said than done – especially for guys (we are not known to be the best communicators). But not everyone may be supportive or understanding.

For me, my faith in God is the most important reason for overcoming the dark, painful times. For a brief time, I left God – God never left me. When I reached out to Him, I received strength and comfort and peace.

Going forward, God blessed me in so many ways. He provided me with a very lucrative career. He led me to a wonderful wife to love. He led me to a church to worship and serve and have amazing fellowship. He has looked after all my children to help them through some very difficult times and give them hope for a bright future. He has given me precious grandchildren – the joy of my life! By God's grace, I have been given a new start in life. And now, I focus my efforts on being an advocate and leader for providing help to those in need. There is much work to be done – research, awareness, education and training, treatment, giving, and serving.

Despite all that is being done, the stigma and the myths continue…

I still remember hearing a preacher say that, "if you can't get over depression, then you don't have enough faith." I was shocked. I want people to know that depression is a disease of the brain and requires treatment. Would you tell someone with a disease like cancer to 'just get over it.'? I don't think so!

Sometimes, the situation gets worse before it gets better. Often, people just don't understand what you are experiencing. Your words may be hurtful – your actions may be strange. You may need to say, "I'm sorry and please forgive me." To those who love you, they need to forgive you and help you.

There is strength in asking for help and having the courage to overcome difficulty (I have been bad about asking for help – always thought that I could do it on my own). I don't advise that at all.

Recently, I saw the movie *Heaven Is For Real*. There was a line in the movie that really hit home for me. Colton, the little boy who had the experience of spending a brief time in heaven, was supported by his dad during the time in which so many doubted. I related to his dad – felt like I had spent a good part of my life standing up for my siblings when others did not understand their illness and needed support and love.

In many ways, I felt like I needed to be the one to save them. As Colton's dad was told, "you don't need to save the world – I think someone has already done that (Jesus)." Really got my attention. It's not about me – it's about them.

****

Usually, there are some very specific things that trigger depression: illness, death of a loved one, divorce, loss of job, financial difficulties, addiction, mental and sexual abuse - even being overwhelmed with life. But there is a big difference between brief, periodic depression (which almost everyone experiences at times) versus chronic depression (which tends to be sustaining and much more debilitating).

Depression is also very intertwined with other mental disorders. When depression sets in, people look for an escape. In one instance, someone may just not feel like getting out of bed in the morning or going anywhere because they can't deal with reality. In the most extreme case, some people commit suicide to end the pain. This is such a tragic act – it not only ends the life of someone who has other options, but it causes unbelievable pain for their family and friends. Suicide is never a good option.

This year, I heard some very tragic news. One of my best friends from grade school had recently committed suicide. I had not seen him or heard from him for many years. He was a super smart guy – became a lawyer and had a lot of friends. I was shocked and deeply disturbed when I heard the way in which he died. How could this happen? Did he reach out to anyone for help? I never could have imagined this happening to my good friend.

As my children have grown up, there have been two instances of suicide among their friends. Both of them were in high school. Suicide among high school students is on the rise; statistics indicate that one in twelve teens in the U.S. attempts suicide. For our current generation of teens, bullying (especially cyber bullying through texting, email, or social media) is a huge cause of stress, rejection, and humiliation which leads to suicide.

But there is always hope. There is always a way to get a new start. There are many wonderful people to help. You may be the one who needs help or it may be someone in your family or a friend. At one time, you may be giving help and at another time you may be the one who needs help.

****

What is happening in our world today?

In August 2014, Lesley Messer of ABC News reported on the death of actor Robin Williams – suspected suicide.

Robin Williams was 63 years old when he died. He was an Oscar-winning actor and comedian. The Marin County Coroner (California) said in a statement, "At this time, the

Sheriff's Office Coroner Division suspects the death to be a suicide due to asphyxia, but a comprehensive investigation must be completed before a final determination is made."

"Robin Williams passed away this morning," Mara Buxbaum, the actor's rep, shared in a statement to ABC News. "He has been battling severe depression of late. This is a tragic and sudden loss

****

What is important to understand is that depression is a common thread in so many illnesses. Some illnesses are physical, some mental, some emotional, and some even spiritual. All of these illnesses can cause depression – not just a brief feeling of sadness, but rather a recurrent feeling of sadness, despair, loneliness, desperation, and hopelessness.

Some of us are predisposed to certain addictions or behavior or types of thinking. It's really hard to understand unless you have lived with this. Because I do understand depression, I have a very different view of life. I am one of the fortunate ones who has been blessed with experiencing a great career and prosperity. Many do not.

Just a few weeks ago, I went to eat lunch at Chick-fil-A. I have always been very impressed with the customer service at this restaurant. Also, the clientele seem to be very friendly people and well mannered. But on this particular day, one customer seemed very out of place.

As I looked outside, there was a man sitting by himself at one of the patio tables. There is no better way to describe him than to say he was clearly a 'homeless guy'. His hair was long and matted, his beard was long and scraggly, his clothes were worn and dirty, and he obviously had not taken a bath for quite some time. But there he was at Chick-fil-A. He had five orders of fries and about ten packages of crackers. He seemed to be in another world – not bothering anyone.

I wondered – what was his story? Did he have a mental disorder? Was he running away from someone? Had he tried to get help and no one responded? What would you do? Would you help?

I do not take anything for granted. I am so thankful for everything that I have. I do not judge anyone because I do not know their circumstances – only God knows. Only God knows their heart. Only God can judge.

For many years, I felt so much sympathy for my great grandma, for Billy, for my Dad, for Kathy, for Mary Ann - because I saw the struggles they had, the relationships that were destroyed, and the rejection they experienced.

I never thought that I would experience rejection the way that I have experienced rejection from family and friends. It made me realize how much people can be misunderstood. People may perceive you as selfish, or rude, or indifferent, or mean, or even violent. Any or all of these behaviors may be demonstrated when people become ill.

For many years, I have observed the way people reacted around Billy and Kathy and Mary Ann. They would stare, they would laugh, or they would shake their head. Many did not understand. They ridiculed or rejected. But a few did understand and care - a few would smile and look at them with love. I never thought that one day I might feel rejected. I had been loved by so many for so long. But that changed.

Because I did things and said things that hurt some people very close to me, I was rejected. I was not loved the same way. Whatever happens in our lives always has consequences – some good and some bad. Some of these consequences may last a lifetime. It doesn't always matter if you try to make up for things that happened in the past. Some people can't forgive – most people never forget.

I have always been someone who wanted to please people. There is some goodness in having this attitude. Typically, I always go above and beyond in whatever I do – whether it's in my professional work or in my personal life. But it also has a downside. Because you will never please everyone all the time no matter how hard you try. It's also easy for others to take advantage of you or to take what you do for granted. Believe me – I learned this the hard way.

Another brutal fact – everyone will disappoint you at some time or another. Even the most loving, caring, and thoughtful people! It's just who we are – humans.

But I am someone who does not give up easily. I believe that everyone can change for the better. I know it is possible. Not because of something I might do or say – but because God touches their heart.

****

About six years ago, I discovered a wonderful organization – Depression and Bipolar Support Alliance Greater Houston (DBSA). This organization provides free and confidential support groups for individuals living with, or family and friends affected by, depression and bipolar disorder. For the past four years, I have served on the Board of Directors for DBSA.

There is an interesting history associated with the organization. During 1979, in response to a critical need expressed by individuals living with depression and bipolar disorders, a group of dedicated individuals formed the Depressive Manic Disorder Association (DMDA) Greater Houston.

In 2003, DMDA Greater Houston changed its name to Depression and Bipolar Support Alliance Greater Houston (DBSA). Led by Gary Levering, a dedicated and enthusiastic participant, DBSA formed its own 501(c) (3) corporation. Gary utilized his personal experience and strong community connections to recruit and build the initial DBSA board of directors, and the Board is still strong and active today

Amazingly, Gary dealt with his own demons of depression and bipolar disorder. But he sought help and got treatment and lived a productive and purposeful life. He led an effort that continues on today to help thousands of people in need. He is a true hero.

Every year, DBSA Greater Houston hosts a luncheon which helps to raise funds and promote awareness in the community. We have a special speaker at the luncheons to share a personal testimony or talk about dealing with mental illness in their family.

There have been some amazing speakers – many of which are very well known as actors and actresses, professional athletes, and professors, including: actress Glenn Close (her sister has been under treatment for depression and schizophrenia); sports legend Terry Bradshaw (he has been under treatment for depression); best-selling author and professor at Johns Hopkins University - Kay Redfield Jamison (she has been under treatment for bipolar disorder).

In addition, there are outstanding clinics to provide patient treatment for mental illness – such as The Menninger Clinic. Menninger is a leading psychiatric hospital dedicated to treating individuals with mood, personality, anxiety and addictive disorders, teaching mental health professionals and advancing mental healthcare through research.

This past year, Menninger hosted a fundraising luncheon. Richard Dreyfuss, well-known actor for many years, was the special speaker. He talked about his struggles with manic depression (bipolar disorder). All of these folks who are well known public figures have displayed tremendous courage and compassion by talking about their mental illness. All these individuals are helping to reduce the stigma associated with mental disorders.

I am so thankful for the many organizations, and their dedicated staff and volunteers that are truly making a difference in the lives of individuals and their families who need help

CHAPTER 11

LIFE IN PRISON:
HOME FOR THE HOMELESS

Myth:
IF THEY'RE IN PRISON, IT'S THEIR FAULT

I received a call from Charlie - one of the pastors at our church. He is very involved in a prison ministry in the Houston area and he asked me to go with him to visit some of the inmates.

Charlie and I have talked about the huge problem of so many people with mental illness who are in prison. Countless men and women never receive the treatment needed – no medication, no counseling, no support groups, no family to care for them.

Even though I had experienced many years of visiting Billy, Kathy, and Mary Ann in residential care homes and seeing some bizarre and upsetting episodes, I had never been in a state prison – much less visited with inmates who were mentally ill.

I was somewhat apprehensive about going but knew that I might be able to meet some men who did not get any visits from family or friends – those who had been abandoned.

As we entered the prison, I followed Charlie's lead. It was a scary feeling – it's very different than what you see on TV or the movies. I could sense the despair, the anger, the loneliness, the pain, and even the evil.

Charlie and I sat down at a table in the visitor area. A man named Jimmy walked over with a guard and sat with us at the table. Jimmy had met with Charlie once before; he looked like he was in his forties – he was very muscular, his teeth were quite yellow and brown, and he stood about 6'3". Charlie had told me that Jimmy seemed to have some type of mental illness and that he was convicted about five years ago for attempted aggravated robbery and received a sentence of ten years in prison. It was his first offense.

I felt a connection with Jimmy almost immediately. He was a kind man. I knew there was something special about him. Jimmy had been on his own since he was 16. His mom and dad were killed in a car accident. He had two older brothers but they had already left the house and had moved away. Jimmy had worked hard on construction crews, but never heard from any of his family.

During our conversation, he kept looking around as if he thought someone might try to hurt him. He told me that he made friends with one of the guards, but did not trust the other inmates – they always made fun of him and called him 'dummy'.

Jimmy had tears in his eyes as he shared stories about life in prison. Many of the inmates were mentally ill and did not get help – no medication or counseling. Many were sexually abused. They were threatened to do things for others just to avoid being hurt. Because Jimmy was big and strong, he was able to defend himself much better. I could see the pain in his eyes and on his face.

****

Suddenly, someone grabbed me and put his arm around my neck. He pulled me up from the table and told everyone to lay on the floor. He held a gun to my head and said that he was going to walk out with me; he would shoot me if anyone tried to stop him.

I prayed to God to help me. I was prepared to die.

A guard lay beside me – unconscious. His gun had been pulled from its holster and now was clutched in the hand of my captor. I have never been so scared in my life. Yet I did not panic.

All eyes focused on us as I was pulled across the room toward the door. No one moved and no one said anything. I felt the gun pressing against my temple and struggled to breathe as his grip tightened against my throat.

As we neared the door, I fell to the ground with my captor falling on top of me. Then I heard a gunshot...

I was a bit dazed - then looked up and saw Jimmy. He said, "It's okay; you're safe now."

Jimmy had come to my rescue. Somehow, he came from behind, grabbed the gun from my captor and pushed him to the ground. No one had been hit when the gun fired. A guard just outside the door rushed in and quickly slapped handcuffs on my captor.

****

I woke up in a cold sweat. What a terrible nightmare! I am so thankful that it was only a nightmare.

Then I realized – for many people, their whole life is a nightmare and they feel as though they are trapped in jail – a mental jail. Every day, there are millions of people who are suffering and scared and lonely. They need help – but so many have no one to help them.

There are also many people who get into trouble with the law because of mental disorders and spend much of their lives behind bars. Instead, they should be receiving treatment for their mental illness in a mental health facility with appropriate security. Even better, we need to provide improved mental healthcare to prevent so many people from getting seriously ill.

CHAPTER 12

THERE IS HOPE

Recently, Lea and I visited St. Louis. We make at least one trip each year to see everyone – especially my sister Kathy and my brothers Billy and John.

Unfortunately, several trips in the past have been to attend funerals – most recently for my sister Mary Ann and for my mom. But this trip would be different – we would be attending a family wedding.

A few months ago, I got an email from my nephew Chris (Mary Ann's youngest son) to let me know that he was getting married. I was so happy to hear from him. The last time I saw him was at his mom's funeral. Since Mary Ann passed away, we have had very little contact with Chris and his brother Noel. I was thrilled that he thought about inviting me and wanted to reconnect with our side of the family.

Chris's bride, Kim, grew up in a very small town in Illinois (Germantown). Kim and Chris had a website for everyone to share in their plans for the wedding and to see photos. It was nice to get updated on how Chris looked and to see what Kim looked like before we would meet her – very beautiful.

As I prepared for the trip, I had many flashbacks about my sister Mary Ann – when times were good and when times were very bad. But most of all, a feeling of peace in knowing that she was now in heaven – no tears, no pain. Now she was able to experience infinite, unconditional love.

On the day of the wedding, we had a good turnout from our side of the family. In addition to Lea and me, other family members attending included my Aunt Jan, my nephew Ryan (John's son) and his girlfriend Makenzi, my cousin Julie and her husband Gary and their two kids, and my cousin Anne and her two kids. My brother John could not attend because he was in severe pain and unable to even leave the house.

We got to the church early so that I could see Chris and give him a big hug before the ceremony. Chris is a rather tall guy (about 6'3"). He was always a bit slender and had a great smile. As I saw him, he had now filled out to be a very handsome, well-built young man and still had that winning smile. His eyes lit up when he saw me. It was a very special moment.

After talking with Chris and Noel and their dad, I went to join the rest of the family to be seated in the church. As we walked into the church building, we met Kim and her family. She looked absolutely gorgeous. I felt close to her the minute that I met her. And her mom and dad and grandparents greeted us warmly and made us feel so welcome.

Before being seated, we picked up a wedding ceremony card. This was to be the first of several very special moments that day. On the card, there were two very touching sections:

Parents of the Groom

NOEL F. AND THE LATE MARY ANN GORCZYCA

In Remembrance

REGRETFULLY, SOME OF OUR FAMILY IS NO LONGER WITH US TO CELEBRATE THIS SPECIAL DAY. WE FEEL THEY ARE HERE IN SPIRIT AND THEY WILL ALWAYS BE IN OUR HEARTS.

Memorable Extras

KIM'S BOUQUET IS WRAPPED IN MARY ANN GORCZYCA'S NECKLACE AND SHE IS WEARING GRAMDMA WESLINGS RING ON HER RIGHT HAND. SHE IS ALSO WEARING A SPECIAL PIECE OF JEWLERY FROM HER AUNT JOYCE.

I broke into tears when I read this – tears of joy. I did not expect anything to be said about Mary Ann at the ceremony. It made my heart glad.

After the wedding ceremony, we had a few hours before the reception would begin. Our family went across the street to a grille for some snacks and drinks. We had a wonderful time catching up, telling some funny stories, and playing the game of 'telephone' to send a message around the group and see what changes by the time it gets all the way around. Needless to say, when there are four young adults ranging from 12-16 in the group, there can be some pretty outlandish things they dream up to say – none of which resemble the original message.

We then left to go to the reception which was about a 15 minute drive from the grille. When we walked into the reception room, it looked beautiful – white lights strewn throughout the entire room. As I looked to my left, I saw a table with a white table cloth.

There was a picture of Mary Ann (her high school graduation picture – she looked so pretty). Beside the picture was a notebook. On the first page were handwritten notes from Kim and Chris.

From Kim:

Mary Ann

Thank you for raising the man I am going to spend the rest of my life with. You brought him into this world, you gave him life, and you shaped him into the gentle, kind-hearted, and caring man that he is today. I have heard many great stories about you which makes me wish even more that I would have met you.

Kim

From Chris:

For those of you who knew my Mom, and for those who didn't, know that she loved conversation. She was a talker. She could make friends with a random lady standing in front of her at McDonald's. It was a gift. And sometimes embarrassing when she introduced Noel and I to the random lady telling her of our latest accomplishments.

My Mom had a great sense of humor. She was entertaining and her laugh and smile were contagious.

There is so much to say, but the thing I love most about my Mom were her hugs. To receive a hug from my Mom was to literally feel as though a polar bear had you in its clasp.

You always made me feel so loved.

Love you always,

Chris

What a special and loving way to honor Mary Ann!

Then, as I looked farther down the table, there was a picture of my Mom ('MeMe' as Chris called her). Along with her picture (in her prime), there was also a notebook with handwritten notes from Kim and Chris.

From Kim:

MeMe,

I have heard so many wonderful stories about how strong of a mother and grandmother you were. I wish I would have had the pleasure of meeting you.

Kim

From Chris:

MeMe,

I have so many wonderful memories of you. You are one of the most courageous and strong women I have ever known, and your sense of humor was unmistakably unique. You always made sure Noel and I had a full belly. And your bedtime back scratches / massages were amazing!

But for me, what stands out more than anything is always feeling loved whenever I was with you. And of course, with that love came the requirement that us grandkids blew kisses and say 'I love you' when we get off the phone. Even as a teenager, and in the presence of my friends, blowing kisses and the 'I love you' were not optional. Embarrassing then, but so worth it to have you as my grandma!

Love Always,

Chris

What a fantastic memorial to MeMe!

I felt so proud of Chris and Kim.

After finding a table and getting settled in, we had the opportunity to meet more of Kim's family. All were very nice people – she obviously comes from a very loving family with strong values.

We enjoyed a wonderful buffet dinner. Of course, my nephew Ryan ate more than anyone (at least twice as much). But he is also the most fit of anyone – burns a lot of calories as a trainer at the gym. Those days are long gone for me.

Next, the wedding party paraded from the back of the room up to the front of the room and were seated so they could face all the rest of the folks. The best man and maid of honor made their speeches – both did a great job. Then they announced the first of several dances which are traditional during the reception – the dance of the bride and groom. Kim and Chris looked very happy as they embraced each other.

Following their dance, Kim and her father (Mark) danced. I could detect the closeness and special father/daughter relationship they shared.

Then they announced the next dance. It was dedicated to Mary Ann. It would have been the dance that Chris would have had with Mary Ann – the mother/son dance. I was speechless.

Chris sat in his chair – everyone sat in their chairs. My eyes swelled with tears. I was overwhelmed by the beautiful, thoughtful, and loving remembrance of Chris's mom – my sister. We listened to the Whitney Houston song – no words, just the music; it was her favorite singing artist.

I will never forget this day. I had no idea that Chris and Kim would do so many special things for Mary Ann. Chris certainly experienced many difficult times during his mom's early years of mental illness. Yet, what he remembers and what he shares with others is the appreciation for all she did in making him feel so loved.

I am so proud to have him as my nephew and feel so happy for him to have found someone as special as Kim.

You never know what impact you may have on people whether they are your family or not. Certainly, my sister Mary Ann had a huge impact on Chris. She struggled in many ways to do the things that other mothers can do – the cooking, cleaning, helping with homework, or working outside the home. But she was a superstar in making her children feel loved.

∗∗∗

Although there are millions of people worldwide who are suffering with some type of mental disorder or intellectual disability, there is hope. There are many people who do care. There are many people who are trying to make a difference by committing themselves to helping others as healthcare professionals or family caregivers or members of support organizations.

Today, you may be the one who will help someone in need and be a hero. Tomorrow, either you or someone in your family may be the one who will need help.

We're all in this together...

NOTE: For updates on how my family is doing today, please read the Epilogue. In addition, please review the Resources section to obtain very valuable information via websites and articles. In particular, please see the sections on Obsessive Compulsive Disorder (OCD), Post-Traumatic Stress Disorder (PTSD), and Autism Spectrum Disorder – all very significant mental disorders but not discussed in my family's story.

THE END

St. Louis State Hospital
Great Grandma Katherine's residence

Mom & Dad (wedding day)

Mary Ann, Billy, Joe (early years)

Billy, Joe, Mary Ann

Janice, Mary Ann, Kathy

Billy, John

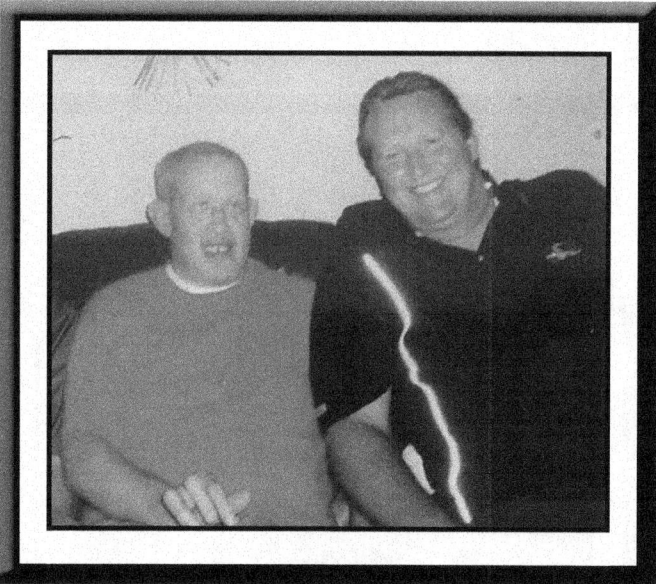

Mom, Uncle Joe, Aunt Rose, Aunt Jan

*1870's clock from my great grandparents;
we've come a long way since that time*

EPILOGUE

Life goes on for our family. We are blessed in so many ways and thankful to so many wonderful people.

Kathy continues to live in a residential group home in Troy, MO. She sees a medical doctor and a psychiatrist on a regular basis. She attends a habilitation program four days per week and takes her medicine every day (Norvasc, Cogentin, Valium, Zyprexa, and Loxapine) as prescribed and she gets a visit from family twice each week (thanks to my aunt Jan and my brother John). The folks at Troy House do a very good job of making sure that Kathy is safe and provided what she needs (thanks to Diana).

Kathy has endured a lot. Despite all her challenges, she hardly ever complains. For her, life is very routine – the simpler the better. She likes to take long walks (keeps her active), listen to her radio (passes the time), drink her coffee (needs to be regulated), and smoke cigarettes (biggest challenge for her to control).

I know that it is very difficult for Kathy to set boundaries – even when she knows what is best. Drinking coffee and smoking cigarettes are very appealing to her – the caffeine helps her overcome the severe drowsiness from all her meds; the nicotine provides a calming effect for her.

Her mental illness (paranoid schizophrenia) is under control and she functions relatively well with the proper care and treatment.

****

Billy continues to live in a residential group home in Bellefontaine, MO. He attends a day program at the facility which allows him to interact with other residents.

Over the years, the care provided to Billy has been up and down. There were some problems that caused me concern. When I would visit Billy, he would not always look healthy or seem to be groomed properly (haircut, shave, clothes). His ear was injured – looked like he had been hit very hard (we were told that one of the residents lost control and hit several of the residents, including Billy).

But the Bellefontaine home has done a wonderful job of making significant improvements. Billy looks absolutely great right now! He seems happier and healthier than ever. And he gets regular visits from family to make sure all is going well for him (thanks to Aunt Antoinette and my cousins Chris and Mike).

Every day, I pray that Kathy and Billy will be safe – that no harm will come to them. I am so thankful to everyone who watches over them.

****

My Uncle Joe has started going to a day program four days a week when Kris is teaching at school. He will have someone to ensure that he is safe and gets his meals and medication.

Generally, he has quit using names to refer to anyone – even those most close to him. He will say 'my daughter' or 'the boyfriend' or 'my sister' or even 'the white little dog'.

When I talk to him, he sounds very happy when I talk about the St. Louis Cardinals baseball team and when we discuss the golf tournaments that he watches on TV.

He is a man with a gentle spirit and a childlike faith. My comfort is knowing that he will be in heaven, where he will know all of us and will no longer be afraid or confused.

****

There have been other significant challenges for our family.

My brother John has dealt with severe chronic pain for over a decade due to a terrible work accident which crushed his spine and feet. He has fallen many times and continually deals with concussions and blood clots.

John reminds me of the Biblical figure Job. He is a good man with strong faith, yet still has endured so much suffering. And he still keeps going – day to day! He is amazing.

But the many years of pain have taken a toll on John. He too has experienced ongoing depression. This is so common for many people who have a chronic physical illness – it also can have an effect mentally and emotionally.

There are others in my family who have various problems – physically, mentally, and emotionally. I have chosen not to write about everyone for reasons that are important to our family at this time.

****

As I look back and reflect, I miss so many of my family who have passed away – my great grandma, my dad, my mom, and Mary Ann.

I am so thankful for the care and love provided for those who have special needs at this time – especially Kathy, Billy, and Uncle Joe.

Because of all that has happened with my family, I don't take anything for granted.

I have been blessed with awesome grandkids – they bring me such joy. It's my way of staying young at heart and just being a big kid who wants to have fun. I never get tired of going to the zoo or the circus, playing hide-and-seek, or building tents in the media room when there are sleepovers. The newest addition is the tree house – a big hit with the kids and adults!

I am so proud when my grandkids take their first steps, say their first words, read their first book, and take their first bike ride. As they are growing up, it is very exciting to go to their soccer games, football games, gymnastics, and school events.

The hugs, the kisses, the tears, and the laughs – keeps me going.

There are times when we all need to make choices. Very important to know your priorities – sometimes they get mixed up. Don't let it happen to you.

Make every day count. Life is too short.

RESOURCES

Mental Health / Mental Illness - General

1. DBSA – Depression and Bipolar Support Alliance

   www.dbsalliance.com

2. Menninger Clinic

   www.menningerclinic.com

3. MHA – Mental Health America

   www.mentalhealthamerica.net

4. NAMI – National Alliance on Mental Illness

   www.nami.org

5. "An Unquiet Mind", Kay Redfield Jamison

6. MentalHealth.gov provides one-stop access to U.S. government mental health resources

   www.mentalhealth.gov

7. NIH – National Institute of Mental Health

   www.nimh.nih.gov/health/find-help/index.shtml

8. Mental Health Resources – Active Minds

   www.activeminds.org/issues-a-resources/mental-health-resources

9. SAMSHA – Substance Abuse and Mental Health Services Administration

www.samhsa.gov/prevention

10. "Diagnosis and Treatment of Mental Disorders Across the Lifespan" Stephanie M. Woo, Carolyn Keatinge

Alcoholism

Alcoholism is an addiction to the consumption of alcoholic liquor or the mental illness and compulsive behavior resulting from alcohol dependency. Alcoholism is often caused by a disease of the brain, characterized by altered brain structure and function.

Resources

1. AA - Alcoholics Anonymous

   www.aa.org

2. Adult Children of Alcoholics

   www.adultchildren.org

3. "Drop the Rock: Removing Character Defects – Steps Six and Seven", Bill Pittman and Todd Weber

4. NIH – National Institute on Alcohol Abuse and Alcoholism

   www.niaaa.nih.gov/

5. Addiction Recovery Programs

   www.recovery.org

Alzheimer's

Alzheimer's disease is an irreversible, progressive brain disorder that slowly destroys memory and thinking skills, and eventually the ability to carry out the simplest tasks. In most people with Alzheimer's, symptoms first appear in their mid-60s. Estimates vary, but experts suggest that more than 5 million Americans may have Alzheimer's.

Resources

1. CNN Film: Glen Campbell – Alzheimer's

    www.cnn.com/shows/glen-campbell-ill-be-me

2. Alzheimer's Association

    www.az.org

3. Alzheimer's Navigator

    www.alzheiimersnavigator.org

4. "The 36-Hour Day: A Family Guide to Caring for People with Alzheimer's Disease, Other Dementias, and Memory Loss in Later Life", Nancy L. Mace and Peter V. Rabins. 4th ed. Baltimore: Johns Hopkins University Press, 2006

5. Alzheimer's Disease Guide: WebMD

    http://www.webmd.com/alzheimers/guide/default.htm

Intellectual Disability

Intellectual Disability, once called mental retardation, is characterized by below-average intelligence or mental ability and a lack of skills necessary for day-to-day living. People with intellectual disabilities can and do learn new skills, but they learn them more slowly. There are varying degrees of intellectual disability, from mild to profound.

Resources

1. AAIDD - American Association on Intellectual and Developmental Disabilities

   www.aaidd.org

2. U.S. Organizations for People with Intellectual Disabilities

   www.clearhelper.org

3. "Intellectual Disability: A Guide for Families and Professionals", James C. Harris, M.D.

4. National Association for persons with Developmental Disabilities

   www.thenadd.org

5. Intermediate Care Facilities

   www.medicaid.gov/medicaid-chip-program-information/by-topics/delivery-systeMs/institutional-care/intermediate-care-facilities-for-individuals-with-intellectual-disabilities-icfid.html

Obsessive Compulsive Disorder

Obsessive–compulsive disorder (OCD) is a mental disorder where people feel the need to check things repeatedly, have certain thoughts repeatedly, or feel they need to perform certain routines repeatedly. People are unable to control either their thoughts or their actions. Common activities include hand washing, counting of things, and checking to see if a door is locked. Some may have difficulty throwing things out. The condition is associated with tics, anxiety disorder, and an increased risk of suicide.

Resources

1. OCD Challenge

   www.ocdchallenge.com

2. International OCD Foundation

   www.iocd.org

3. The Menninger Clinic

   www.menningerclinic.com

4. OCD Organizations and Support Groups

   www.geonius.com/ocd/organizations.html

5. "The Man Who Couldn't Stop: OCD and the True Story of a Life Lost in Thought" by David Adam

Post-Traumatic Stress Disorder

Post-traumatic stress disorder (PTSD) is a mental disorder that can develop after a person is exposed to a traumatic event, such as sexual assault, warfare, traffic collisions, or other threats on a person's life. Symptoms may include disturbing thoughts, feelings, or dreams related to the events, mental or physical distress, attempts to avoid trauma-related cues, alterations in how a person thinks and feels, and increased arousal. Those with PTSD are at a higher risk of suicide.

Resources

1. NIH: National Institute of Mental Health – PTSD
   www.nimh.nih.gov/health/topics/post-traumatic-stress
   disorder-ptsd/index.shtml

2. Veterans Crisis Line
   Call: 1-800-273-8255, or text at 838255 24 hours a day,
   seven days a week. There's also information online at
   www.ptsd.va.gov

3. Mayo Clinic: Post-traumatic stress disorder
   www.mayoclinic.org/diseases-conditions/post-traumatic-
   stress-disorder/basics/definition/con-20022540

4. Women's Voices for Change: PTSD-Condition affects
   significant number of women
   http://womensvoicesforchange.org/post-traumatic-
   stress-disorder-condition-affects-significant-number-
   of-women.htm

5. 'Buddy Check on 22!' Veterans Use Social Media to Fight
   Suicide April 2016, Christine Hauser, New York Times

Autism Spectrum Disorder

Autism is a neurodevelopmental disorder characterized by impaired social interaction, verbal and non-verbal communication, and restricted and repetitive behavior. Parents usually notice signs in the first two years of their child's life. These signs often develop gradually, though some children with autism reach their developmental milestones at a normal pace and then regress.

Resources

1. Autism Spectrum Disorders: WebMD

   http://www.webmd.com/brain/autism/autism-spectrum-disorders

2. Autism Society

   http://www.autism-society.org/what-is/aspergers-syndrome/

3. ASPEN: Autism Spectrum Education Network

   http://aspennj.org/what-is-asperger-syndrome

4. National Autism Center: For Families

   www.nationalautismcenter.org/resources/for-families/

5. Rising Autism Prevalence 'driven by changes in classification' July 2015, David McNamee, Medical News

Acknowledgements

The following news reports and articles were referenced to provide insight on specific events that are happening in the world today related to mental disorders.

1. Prison Problem: Our Mentally Ill
    March, 2015, Mark Joyella, TV Newser

2. Horrific conditions still exist in some mental health facilities
    April 2015, Nicholas Perpitch, ABC News – Australia

3. Students face charges for raping mentally disabled girl
    June 2015, Christina Veiga, Miami Herald

4. Drunk Drivers in America
    July 2015, Hoda Kotb, NBC News: Dateline

5. Schizophrenic man shot by police
    March 2015, Eliott C. McLaughlin, CNN

6. Mentally ill man opens fire at elementary school
    December 2012, Richard A. Friedman, New York Times

7. Elderly woman with Alzheimer's is missing
    August 2015, Amie Schaenzer, Libertyville Patch (IL)

8. Actor Robin Williams is dead of suspected suicide
    August 2014, Lesley Messer, ABC News

CALL TO ACTION

Most people want to leave a great legacy.

For some, it may be a legacy of fame, fortune, or power. For others, it may be a legacy of courage, service, or sacrifice.

I hope to leave a legacy of compassion, gratitude, and giving:

- Compassion for the millions of people who live with mental disorders and intellectual disability.

- Gratitude for all the family, friends, psychiatrists, psychologists, nurses, counselors, teachers and mental healthcare professionals who serve those in need

- Giving back through service and donations to the Depression and Bipolar Support Alliance, National Alliance on Mental Illness, Special Olympics, and United Way.

My family has dealt with an incredible number of mental disorders. I feel extremely blessed to be part of this family because I have experienced unconditional love – both given and received.

My call to action for everyone who reads this book: make a difference for good in the life of someone who really needs you. Help to stop the stigma related to mental disorders. Let's find a better way to stop the pain and give hope to the millions of people who are hurting.

If you are struggling with a mental disorder, tell someone. If you know someone needs help, get them help. There are many caring people and many dedicated organizations that want to help.

There is a way to a better life. There is hope.

Request from the author

I need your help!

Please share your feedback with me.

I would also like to hear your story.

Email: joe_gorczyca@yahoo.com

Website: www.joegorczyca-brainpain.com

With heartfelt thanks,

Joe Gorczyca

www.ingramcontent.com/pod-product-compliance
Lightning Source LLC
Chambersburg PA
CBHW061723020426
42331CB00006B/1063